A Model For Life

A Proven Technique for Purposeful and Successful Living

Frank S.D. Alexander, B.A., M.Ed.

Order this book online at www.trafford.com/08-1297
or email orders@trafford.com

Most Trafford titles are also available at major online book retailers.

Cover Design by: Dwight Alexander

Note for Librarians: A cataloguing record for this book is available from Library and Archives Canada at www.collectionscanada.ca/amicus/index-e.html

ISBN: 978-1-4251-8805-4

We at Trafford believe that it is the responsibility of us all, as both individuals and corporations, to make choices that are environmentally and socially sound. You, in turn, are supporting this responsible conduct each time you purchase a Trafford book, or make use of our publishing services. To find out how you are helping, please visit www.trafford.com/responsiblepublishing.html

Our mission is to efficiently provide the world's finest, most comprehensive book publishing service, enabling every author to experience success. To find out how to publish your book, your way, and have it available worldwide, visit us online at www.trafford.com/10510

www.trafford.com

North America & international
toll-free: 1 888 232 4444 (USA & Canada)
phone: 250 383 6864 • fax: 250 383 6804
email: info@trafford.com

The United Kingdom & Europe
phone: +44 (0)1865 487 395 • local rate: 0845 230 9601
facsimile: +44 (0)1865 481 507 • email: info.uk@trafford.com

10 9 8 7 6 5 4 3 2

To my mom: The Nonpareil of Women

Table of Contents

Introduction

This book is a sure-fire guide to a purposeful and successful life.

It demonstrates that success is never easier, never more fulfilling, more lasting, than when the journey toward success is rooted in faith.

In response to Rick Warren's encouragement in The Purpose Driven® Life, the book is written to provide a layman's account of how success is achieved through faith.

It is a conversation between a father and his son. It is the result of the son's request of his dad to record the secrets of his success, so that the son would not forget them, and so would be able to use them as a roadmap to his own success.

The conversation between father and son starts on a cool spring morning and lasts well into the evening. In it the dad provides his son with a treasure trove of techniques for success.

Anchoring the book are ten simple rules for success.

When followed, the rules yield incredible blessings and rewards.

At the end of the book are Appendices, with practical exercises on each chapter. The exercises allow the reader to identify life skills gaps. The reader then has an opportunity to create an action plan to do the necessary things to close the identified gaps.

The lessons learned from the book will lead the reader to a purposeful and successful life.

Prologue

Standing on the front porch in the cool spring air, Tommy stares into the distance at nothing in particular. A gentle breeze brushes his face and causes the nearby evergreens to rustle. The trees stand erect, like sentinels on duty, only momentarily nodding to the passing breeze then springing back to attention.

He planted those trees. Yet, somehow they seem to have taken on a life of their own and grown with an air of certitude about their place in the garden, nay, in the world.

They seem at home in this rhythm of nature. They question nothing, yet seem to know everything. Like the manner in which they bowed to the passing breeze, as to a friend, when they know each other so well, that a nod of the head is all the greeting that's necessary.

If only he had been this certain of his place in the world, thought Tommy. If only he had that thing that the evergreens and the wind possess. He would know implicitly what to do and when to do it; without worry and without trepidation. Maybe there is a lesson here somewhere, but.... His thoughts were abruptly interrupted by a cacophony of sound in the distance. As the noise drew closer he recognized it as the raucous sounds of a gaggle of Canada geese on their return journey from the south. In the still of the morning the honking sounded louder than ever. Tommy jumped off his porch and ran to the fence to the east, to see whether he could catch a glimpse of the returning travelers. Before long he had a front row view to a magnificent spring spectacle. The geese, in a giant "V" formation suddenly appeared from behind the houses in the distance and made their way directly over where Tommy stood. With rhythmic strokes they cut the cool spring air, and as they passed above, Tommy could hear the "swoosh" of their wings as they purposefully headed west on their triumphant and celebratory return. What a sight thought Tommy! The tightness of their formation, the rhythm of their wings was truly amazing. But more amazing was the purposefulness of their flight. They knew where they were going, just as they knew when to leave, last fall, and when to return this spring. Awesome!

To have such knowledge must be true bliss. If only he had such knowledge, Tommy thought. If only he knew how to at least ask the questions in his youth, he might have been able to find the answers, like the evergreens, the wind and the geese.

It's too late now, he thought. In the twilight of his years and with retirement on the horizon, the questions seemed to have arrived too late.

"Hey dad", said Pierre. Tommy turns to see his son Pierre approaching.

"Hey Pierre", Tommy replied. "You're up early", continued Tommy.

"Yeah, somehow I couldn't sleep late today", Pierre replied. "You're up early too, what are you doing?" asked Pierre.

"Just enjoying the spring air and thinking", Tommy replied.

"Thinking about what?" Pierre asked.

"About retirement. Maybe in three years I could pack it all in and take a break", Tommy replied.

"What will you do with your time?" Pierre asked.

"I don't know" replied Tommy. "I haven't thought that far ahead".

"Why not write a book?" Pierre asked.

"A book about what?" asked Tommy.

"I don't know, how about the stuff we talk about all the time; about life, and plans and decisions and those life

lessons you talk about; that would be nice to share," Pierre responded.
"Oh I don't know, son; talking is one thing, writing is something completely different. When we talk we don't plan anything. We don't discuss things in any particular order; as they come up we chat. And as you know, we meander from topic to topic. Writing is different. You have to have things follow a certain order, to abide by a certain discipline. I don't think I have that kind of discipline. Besides, who would want to hear what I have to say?" Tommy continued.
"I would", Pierre countered. "Maybe if you write them down, I won't forget them. Besides, I think a book would be a good keepsake for me as I grow up," Pierre replied. "Write it just as we talk. Call it: 'Dad's words of wisdom' or 'Dad's Experiences', anything at all, but I think you should write something".
"Alright, I'll think about it. But if I do write, where would you like me to start?" Tommy asked.
"How about your experiences growing up; how you lived back then, the kinds of things you did growing up and what shaped your life", Pierre responded.
Tommy thought for a moment about what Pierre had said and thought to himself: 'maybe Pierre is right. Maybe there is some wisdom I can share with him so that he could avoid some of my pitfalls over the years. Without a teacher or mentor it's certainly difficult to make sense of things, especially for a young person. Maybe Pierre has a point; even if it means nothing to anyone else, it certainly means something to him. So maybe I'll give some thought to writing that book'.
Tommy then turns to Pierre and says: "You know what son, I'll take up your suggestion. I'll write the book. But let's go and sit on the porch and talk about some of the things you would like me to write about."

Together they walked back to the porch and sat on the steps in momentary silence. Until now Tommy had not stopped to reflect on his life. The prodding of his son suddenly made him realize that maybe, just maybe, he might have something to say.

It seemed so long ago though; growing up in the small village…

“What are you thinking about dad?” Pierre asked.

“I was thinking about growing up in Mt. Rose, how that place shaped me and how much of Mt. Rose is still in me”, Tommy replied.

“Was growing up in Mt. Rose tough on you?” asked Pierre.

“In retrospect, yes” his dad replied.

“What was it like?” asked Pierre.

“As you know I grew up without a father. He left home when I was about three or four and so I grew up without a father figure around”, Tommy continued.

“That must have been tough”, said Pierre, “because I couldn’t imagine growing up without you”.

“Thanks son. Yeah, it was rough, but I had the greatest mom that one could have. Every thing that I know she taught me. All the values I have, she instilled in me. She taught me to live life from the inside out.”

“What do you mean?” asked Pierre.

Chapter 1

Life From The Inside Out

"It was her approach to every aspect of her life, from the break of day to the close of night. At five o'clock each morning mom would wake us up to pray. She would gather my sisters and brother and me around her bed where we would all kneel and pray. Every day began the same way, and ended the same way. And although I didn't realize it then, God became the centre of our existence. We started each day with Him, before we began our own day. We started from the inside out. What my mom was teaching us then was that everything begins with God. As I thought about it later in life I realized that even God practiced this approach. When He made the world, He started with Himself. Jesus too used this approach as did Moses.
When Jesus's disciples asked him: 'Lord, teach us to pray', Jesus replied, 'When you pray, say:

'Our Father who art in heaven,
Hallowed be thy name.
Thy kingdom come,
Thy will be done,
On earth as it is in heaven.
Give us this day our daily bread;
And forgive us our debts, as we also have forgiven our Debtors;
And lead us not into temptation,
But deliver us from evil.' [Matthew 6:9-13][1]

He taught them to start with God.
In Old Testament times when Moses needed answers to a question, invariably his approach was 'Let me inquire

of the Lord…' He always started with God – from the inside out.
Over time I came to realize that if I am to have success in any endeavour, or in life itself, I must always begin from the inside out. When you do things from the inside out, you begin with God, then yourself then those around you. Like a pebble dropped in a pool, the greatest impact is at the centre first, and then it spreads beyond the centre to further influence its surroundings."
"I am not sure I understand what you mean", said Pierre.
"Let me explain further", Tommy responded. "When you live life from the inside out, you tend, for example, not to blame others for your misfortune – because first, you look at yourself to see what you could do before looking to others. If you are in an untenable situation, you first look to see what changes you could make before looking outside. If you have goals to achieve, you first look to see what you could do to achieve them, before looking elsewhere. But always, before you look to yourself, you first go to the Lord in prayer. Then you truly live from the inside out, and position yourself to succeed at all you set out to do.
Life becomes difficult when we live it from the "outside in", Tommy continued. "If, for example, people outside your family think of you more highly than those within your family, then you are living from the outside in. If others see you as loving, kind and helpful, yet those in your immediate family cannot say the same, then you are living from the outside in. When that happens, trouble is not too far from your door.
My father lived life from the outside in. Neighbours, friends and acquaintances always had great praise for him and saw him as a 'good man'. Yet that 'good man' had left his family in dire straits, even as he helped families not his own.

Needless to say, living life from the "outside in" leads to failure. Living life from the inside out leads to incredible success. It is a fundamental requirement for success and it begins with loving God. As Jesus said to a scribe:…'you shall love the Lord your God with all your heart, and with all your soul, and with all your mind, and with all your strength.' [And] 'You shall love your neighbour as yourself.'
[Mark 12:28-30][2]
Some people mistakenly believe that first you start with God, then your neighbour, then yourself. But when you look at Jesus's words closely they reveal that after loving God, you must then love yourself, then your neighbour. Love from the "inside out"; from God outward. Everything starts with God".[3]

Getting My Head Around God

"Over the years as I looked at all God had created using this approach, I couldn't help but think: 'If God used and uses this approach, then surely this must be a true model for life'."
"Did you always know that dad?" asked Pierre.
"Oh no, not by a long shot. That understanding came years later", Tommy replied.
"When I was young I had difficulty understanding this concept. I had trouble getting my head around God. In the early days when we prayed with mom, I prayed by rote. I repeated the prayers I was taught. As I grew older, in my teen years I sought a greater connection between my prayers and the person to whom I prayed. I tried to find some focus for my prayers – a face, a shape, anything; but I couldn't.
Some days I would look up at the sky with this incredible sense of helplessness at the enormity of the chasm that lay between God and me, trying to find

some way to reach Him in thought and word, but couldn't. I didn't know how.

I later learned that this quest of mine to know God more intimately was not unique to me. It is a challenge that each one who seeks God goes through in one form or another.

For me it was doubly difficult, because I had no one to teach me in a way I could understand. As human beings in order to understand anything we need to define it in order to be able to understand it. That's why we name things. The moment you name something or someone, you freeze them at a point in time and space, which then allows you to know and understand.

That's why I struggled to get my head around God. I had neither seen God nor heard God, nor had I been given a description of Him, so it was difficult to address Him. What I in effect was trying to do was the impossibly futile task of limiting God so I could understand Him.

I was relieved to learn later in life that I was not the only one to struggle with God.

When God was recruiting Moses to lead God's people out of Egypt, Moses wanted to nail down who God was so that his report to the people of Israel could be credible. So when God put the proposition to Moses to act as leader of God's people, Moses asked Him: "If I come to the people of Israel and say to them, 'The God of your fathers has sent me to you,' and they ask me, 'What is his name?' What shall I say to them?" God said to Moses, 'I AM WHO I AM." [Exodus 3:13-14][4]

Moses was in part trying to get his head around God; to reduce Him to a level at which he could understand, and at which he could make the people of Israel understand, but God would not, could not be so limited.

Moses's difficulty was my difficulty. I was trying to know God with my head in stead of my heart. Not only that, I made the mistake of trying to reach God without an intermediary."

"Did you ever move from your head to your heart?" Pierre asked.

"It took me a while, but I eventually did," Tommy replied.

"How did you do it?" Pierre asked.

"I began by observing my mom." Tommy replied. "You see", he continued, "When I was growing up we didn't have very much. In fact there were days when we didn't know where the next meal was going to come from. Those days were heart-wrenching for my mom. Every now and then I would see her crying inconsolably. It got so unbearable at times that she would shout at the top of her voice: 'Jesus son of David have mercy on me! Jesus son of David, have mercy on me! Son of David, have mercy on me!'

Three times she would shout. Invariably, at the end of her shouting, a peace would descend upon her, and all would be made right."

Getting My Head Around Jesus

"At that young age, about five or six, I began to make the connection between Jesus and prayer; Jesus and help; Jesus and relief.

Jesus I could now get my head around and my heart too.

Because he once was a man – a form I could conceive of and whose actions I could in some small way understand – the distance between my head and my heart got a little shorter.

The relief he brought my mom tied my heart to him, and later, the relief and support he brought me, tied my heart to him forever."

"How did you come to develop that relationship?" asked Pierre.

"There were two memorable occasions in my youth that helped me. The first was an incident that took place with my mom. The second was an incident that affected me directly.

One day at Christmastime, mom was getting ready to prepare the Christmas meal and needed some fruits to complement the dish she was making. I was sitting on the front steps when she called to me: 'Tommy' she said, 'go to the garden and bring me some bananas.' What struck me then was the certainty with which mom spoke. She didn't say: 'Tommy, go to the garden and see whether you find some bananas' but rather, 'bring me some bananas'.

Our house was on a small farm, of about an acre. So I took my machete and scoured the entire area looking for bananas, but found none. After a while, I returned to mom and said, 'I didn't find any mom'. She said to me, 'Go look again'.

Again I went, this time taking more time to ensure that I had thoroughly searched the field. Finding nothing, I returned to mom again and said, 'I didn't find any mom'. She said to me, 'go look one more time'.

Again I went, this time spending even more time searching, making sure that I didn't miss anything. To my chagrin, I found nothing. Disappointed, I turned toward the house to give mom the bad news. Just as I was about to leave the field to return to the house, I smelt something; it smelt like ripe or ripening bananas. I stopped suddenly, sniffed the air, and walked in the direction from which I thought the smell was coming. As I drew closer, the smell got stronger.

I arrived at what appeared to me to be the scrawniest looking banana tree. It was thin, looked mal-nourished, and had grown taller than most banana trees grow. I

slowly raised my eyes and looked up the tree to where bananas would normally hang; and sure enough, against the sky was a small, partly ripe, bunch of bananas, caught up in a thorn tree.
With excitement at having indeed found bananas, I cut the tree with my machete to retrieve the bananas. Alas, because it was caught up in the branches, it didn't fall, and I couldn't reach it. I eventually tied my machete to a bamboo pole and dislodged the bananas.
Triumphantly I returned to mom and handed her the bananas. With a knowing smile she thanked me, and went on to prepare one of the most delicious and memorable Christmas meals I ever had.
What struck me about that experience was the conviction that mom showed about the existence of bananas in the field. It's not that she knew there was, it was that she was certain there would be. It was as if she had prayed as she always did for help with the meal, and knew that Jesus would not let her down.
As you can tell, I have never forgotten that experience. It was something that always amazed me about mom. In all things, she carried herself in a way that you always knew that she knew. In later years I began to realize that she was indeed the epitome of faith. She walked with "the assurance of things hoped for, the conviction of things not seen.' [Hebrews 11:1].*5*
"And how do you get to that place?" Pierre asked.
"For me it began with observing my mom and pondering in my heart and turning over in my mind, those things I observed in her. I questioned and wondered and yearned to be like her. I became a good observer of life and nature, questioning things and trying to find answers and God in all things.
I believe that's how it must start. As you question things, as you wonder about things, God eventually leads you to the answers. And slowly, over time,

through a combination of your questioning and searching, He provides evidence of His reality and existence.
That happened to me on the second memorable occasion I mentioned earlier; while I attended Elementary school."

Getting My Heart Around Jesus

"As I made my way through elementary school, my hope was to one day make it to high school. It was a hope, because in those days entering high school was not automatic. In the first place there was only one Christian boys' high school serving the entire island, so that meant that competition to get in was tough. Secondly, you had to pass an entrance exam to get in. And even if you made it in, your parents had to be able to pay the fees that were mandatory in those days. So the odds were stacked against me: I didn't think I was bright enough to compete, and my mom couldn't afford the fees.
There was, however, one small window of opportunity. If you could pass the scholarship exams, then your high school education would be free. That was my only hope – getting a scholarship.
The scholarship exams were set at two stages during elementary school – one was set before you were twelve years old - 'an under- twelve scholarship'. The final one was set before you were fourteen 'an under-fourteen scholarship'. If you failed them both, your only hope was to then compete for a fee-paying place through a common entrance exam. If you failed that, you simply left elementary school and found a job.
The stakes for me were therefore very high. Nothing was more important to me than an education. I loved to learn. I was a voracious reader and found excitement in

knowing things. If I wanted to continue my love of learning therefore, I had to get to high school.

In my eleventh year, I prepared for and sat the 'under-twelve scholarship' exam. I failed it. The next two years, I worked as hard as I could, and in my thirteenth year, I prepared for and sat the 'under- fourteen scholarship' exam. I failed it also. My hopes of continuing my dream began to fade.

A year earlier my mom scraped together some money and bought me a calf. I named her Meggy. Her coat was like that of burnished gold. It had some dark stripes that looked like they would befit a Bengal tiger. She had large mischievous eyes and long thin legs. Her gaunt frame exposed ribs in dire need of being covered up with some fat. Meggy and I took to each other right away and I set out to care for her and to fatten her.

Although I didn't know it then, what mom was doing for me was preparing a contingency plan. Her hope was that if I was unsuccessful in getting a scholarship, I would be able to rear that animal, and maybe she would have calves of her own, thereby providing the seed money for me to start school, should I pass the common entrance exam. At the very least, if she didn't have calves, we would be able to sell her for the seed money.

So in the intervening years I cared for my calf. She grew from a thin mal-nourished looking calf, into a beautiful and healthy cow. Even as I cared for her and nurtured her, I prepared for my last remaining opportunity to enter high school – sitting and passing the common entrance exam.

My mom worked diligently with me, teaching me and preparing me for that big day.

The night before I was to sit the common entrance exam, we said our prayers as was customary. During prayers I remember mom asking Jesus to help me with my exam the following day. I said 'good night' to mom and got into bed to get some sleep as I had to get up early the next morning to catch the bus to the city to write the exam.

I was just about to fall asleep when mom called from the living room. I got out of bed and went to her. As I entered the living room she said to me, 'Let's just do a few examples of math and language arts questions for tomorrow.' I looked on the living room wall, which she often used as a 'black board', and there she had set out some math and language questions.

I worked through the questions, late into the night, with mom helping me where I was having difficulty. After it was all done, I bid mom goodnight, and tired, crawled into bed and went to sleep.

At five o'clock the next morning mom roused me. As usual, we all knelt around her bed to say our morning prayers. While we prayed, she again asked Jesus to bless me and to grant me success in my entrance exams. After prayers, as was customary, I tended to Meggy, had a shower, had breakfast, got dressed and waited on the bus that was to take me to the city to write the exams. After what seemed like an eternity the bus came. I kissed mom goodbye and boarded it.

As I sat on that bus on my way to Grenville, my stomach was in knots. As we meandered our way along the narrow roads of Mt. Rose, the pace of everything seemed to quicken. My heart beat faster than usual. The trees rushed by as the bus raced down the serpentine and precipitous hills of Pointsfield, with its passengers sliding from side to side along the wooden seats with each twist and turn along the road. It stopped briefly in Tivoli to pick up passengers, then sped toward Grenville, bounding over the Paradise Bridge, and arriving breathlessly at the Grenville Market Square. Upon arriving at Grenville, I alighted from the bus and walked the short distance to the examination hall, located in an elementary school. The school was a large brick building, with wide steps and stained glass windows. It was called the Old Church School, because it was once a church, now converted to a school.

My legs could hardly carry me as I ascended the steps. My heart pounded so loudly, I could hear it echo in my ears. As I reached the top landing, I pulled open the large mahogany doors and entered. As I walked in, I saw row upon row of tables and chairs neatly arranged in straight lines throughout the room.

I was among the first to arrive. The exams were to start at nine o'clock, and I arrived at eight o'clock. I walked toward the registration table and gave my name. The receptionist scanned the list of names and checked off mine. She then led me to a table and chair and I sat down. On the table was the exam paper face down. Beside it were pens and writing paper. I was asked not to touch anything and not to start writing, until advised to do so. Nine o'clock finally came. 'You may now begin,' said the proctor.

With trembling hands I picked up the examination paper and turned it over. In an instant my fear and trepidation turned to joy. The language arts questions which were first on the page were of the type that mom had prepared for me the night before. I quickly turned to the math section, and there too the math questions were of the type that mom had prepared and helped me with the previous night! I had trouble containing my joy. My hands that only moments ago trembled in fear now trembled with excitement.

With some effort I contained myself, calmed my nerves, and began writing. I was oblivious to all around me as I wrote. I only 'came to' toward the end when the proctor's voice boomed from somewhere within the room: 'fifteen more minutes!' I quickly wrapped up what I was doing, re-read what I had done and finished within the allotted time.

'Pens down', said the proctor. Everyone stopped writing. The receptionist came around and gathered all the papers, then we left.

I bounded down the Old Church steps and raced toward the bus terminal to board the bus to return home. I couldn't wait to give mom the good news. The ride home was in complete contrast to my morning ride. Now everything seemed slower. The bus seemed to stop more frequently; the trees seemed to pass in slow motion. A profound calm enveloped me and a joy settled in my heart.

As the bus neared my stop, unbridled joy burst from my heart. The bus barely came to a stop when I jumped out and raced up the driveway shouting: 'Mom! Mom!'

Mom was in the living room as I burst through the door. Breathlessly I related to her all that had happened. With that knowing smile, she opened her arms and embraced me and softly said, 'You're going to high school'.

The wait between writing the exams and receiving a response seemed interminable. Then one day, about a month later, the postman arrived. He had only one letter to deliver that day; the one from the high school. Afraid to open it, I handed it to mom. As she opened it, I stared intently at her face. As she began to silently read it, a smile broke her face and she handed it to me. It was an acceptance letter. I was going to high school.

Throughout that entire day I recounted the events leading up to my acceptance: the disappointments at the scholarships, the preparation mom put me through; the specific help she requested for me in prayer; the answer to those prayers on entrance exam day and then the acceptance.

It was the first time I had experienced the reality of prayer and God's response to prayer; for now that reality had touched me. I could now make the connection. It was on that day that I first believed. It was on that day that I realized that Jesus is real and that God is real."

"Is that why you only pray to Jesus?" asked Pierre.

"Only to him and only through to him to his Father", Tommy replied.

"Why only him?" asked Pierre.

"He is the only one who has earned the right", replied Tommy. "He is the only one who suffered for me, died for me and redeemed me", Tommy continued. "To go to or through any one else would be an affront to and rejection of his sacrifice. In fact he has made it clear that no one can go to his Father, except through him. In retrospect, that was part of my problem when I was having trouble getting my head around God. I didn't know that I couldn't reach the Father, except through the son.

Even in the early days, in the days of Moses, no one with any blemishes could approach God. All offerings made to Him had to be without blemish; so only the pure of heart and pure of spirit could approach Him directly. And here I was, a blemished heart and blemished spirit, wanting to approach Him directly. But I didn't have that knowledge then; until he led me to his son.

When I finally discovered the right channel for my prayers, I set out to develop a relationship with Jesus. He is able to take my imperfect prayers and blemished heart and make them acceptable to his Father. When he delivered for me on that entrance exam day, that sealed my commitment to him."

"When you declared your commitment to Jesus did it take you a while to establish your relationship with him?" asked Pierre.

"It did. For a long time I learned about him but didn't know him. It wasn't until I understood the rules governing that relationship that our relationship grew and blossomed."

"What do you mean?" Pierre asked.

"Take your friend Jose; you are best friends, right?"

"Yes".

"There are, for example, things you both talk about and things that you don't, because they are taboo right?"

"Right".

"Those things that you talk about and the things that you don't are all governed by a set of rules, both spoken and unspoken. And although you have never written them down, you both know implicitly, anytime either of you crosses the line. These rules are boundaries set around that relationship and which make it successful. I also found that as I got to know Jesus I realized that our relationship was also governed by a set of rules."

"Don't tell me!" Pierre exclaimed. "It's the Commandments, right?"

"Exactly. I found that as long as I stayed within the boundaries of the Commandments, our relationship grew richer and richer, and I knew him better and better. Anytime I crossed the line, we grew apart. Once I established that the Commandments were the foundation of my relationship with Jesus, I then actively sought to live within them, as well as look for ways to shore up and enrich our relationship.

Now each day I find validation of his existence, and delight in finding him in all of God's creation. And I delight in bringing you and your brother and sister and others to a relationship with Jesus; because to get your head around God, you must first get your head around Jesus. You must look for, and you will certainly find, connections between your day-to-day reality and his

existence. For only when you are able to make that personal connection, does God become real."
"I know you help us make that connection", said Pierre. "And I find that the more I try, the easier it becomes and the deeper the connection. But that only becomes easier for us as we talk with you and ask questions about every-day things," said Pierre.

Chapter 2

The Real Life Connection

What Kids Need To Know

"One of the turning points about God's presence and reality in our every-day lives came for me as I listened to a speech you gave one day to a grade eight graduating class. I didn't know about the 'inside-out' principle then, but having talked to you about it on many occasions since, I now realize how much of that speech encompassed all we have been talking about this morning: beginning all things with God, and making Jesus an integral part of our daily lives. Do you remember what you said to them then?" asked Pierre. "Vividly," Tommy responded. "I even remember how I came to write it. In the lead up to the graduation I remember asking Jesus: 'Lord, what do you want me to say to your kids this season?' Before that day ended it occurred to me that I should both demonstrate the 'inside-out' principle, as well as help the children understand how to engage Jesus in the next phase of their lives. The inspiration for those words certainly came from Jesus and not from me. This is what I said in part:

As you leave Ecole Marguerite Bourgeoys, do not forget what you have learned. Continue on your road to success by doing, as Mother Teresa advised, "small things with great love". For when you do small things with great love, you learn how to do great things with great love.

So practice small things with great love first at home, then at school, then the community and later your country and the world. Like a stone dropped in a pool, make a difference where you are and let the ripple effect of your good works spread outward. And here let me take some liberty with Mother Teresa's poem: "Do it anyway" to demonstrate.

When Nana has difficulty opening her pill bottle, and doesn't ask you for help because she wants to be independent, help her anyway.

When Grandpa takes his cane to go for his evening walk - although he doesn't ask you to - walk with him anyway.

When Mom, after a hard day's work is busy making supper while your little sister or brother is tugging at her apron to get attention – although she does not ask for your help – help her anyway.

When Dad cuts the grass and is raking the grass clippings – although he doesn't ask for your help – help him anyway. You see, when you do such small things with great love, you are honoring Mom, Dad, Grandma and Grandpa. And in honoring them, you take the first step to guaranteeing your future success. Here is why: God has made you this promise: If you honor your mother and father, not only will you live a long time, but you will also be prosperous. So see that you do small things with great love at home.

Every now and then I think about your futures. I think about the great things that await you. I think about the great things you will do.

I think too about how important each and every one of you is to this world. How God in His wisdom, thought you important enough, good enough, smart enough, to give you a place on this earth. With such a vote of confidence, all you have to do is seize this gift of life and make it worthwhile.

I think about how, just as He sent His son to do His will, He has sent each of you to His will also.

Some of you He has sent to be Doctors. Some of you Lawyers. Some of you Teachers.

But whatever He has sent you to do; He only asks that you accept His mission for you as Jesus did his.
He asks that you obey Him in all things. He asks that you be excellent in all you do. He asks that you use all His talents, and be as versatile as you can be.

He asks that you keep in touch regularly, to ensure that you are on the right track. He asks that you love one another. He asks that you have Faith in him and know that He will take you safely to wherever he sends you.

And every now and then I think about the challenges you will face. How you are growing up in a world where right will be made to seem wrong and wrong seem right.
How you will face a world that emphasizes commitment to self rather than commitment to others.

How Technology and Science will seek to diminish Faith. Yes, there will be challenges. But you have been, and will be well prepared to face the challenges. God has blessed you with good parents and good teachers and an excellent support system.

There will be times when you will falter. There will be times when you will stumble and fall. There will be times when you will feel uncertain about the future.

But take comfort in this: "behind the unknown standeth God within the shadows, keeping watch above His own". And you are all God's own.

He has endowed you with Faith. A Faith nurtured at home, nurtured at church and shaped at Ecole Marguerite Bourgeoys.

So take this precious gift with you wherever you may go. Use it as a light to guide you in the dark. As a staff if you should stumble.

For with this Faith you will be able to climb the highest mountain and swim the widest ocean.

With this faith, you will be able to ask of the father all that you need to succeed and He will grant it.
With this faith you will be able to face an uncertain world with a renewed sense of confidence.

So as you make your way to high school take this faith with you. And any time you feel down or in need of help, in Faith ask the Father through the son.

If you ask the son, He will show you how to deal with the challenges of High School. He will show you how to succeed at Chemistry, at Language Arts, at Math, at Shop, at Botany, at Biology, at Physics; at whatever you choose to do.

And some of you are probably wondering – can Jesus really do that? The answer is an unequivocal "yes!"

For you see, when you can turn water into wine, you must know more about Chemistry than any one who has walked this earth.

When you can deliver a Sermon on the Mount without notes, without microphone and without a Teleprompter, you must know more about Language Arts than anyone who has walked this earth.

When you can take five loaves and two fish and feed five thousand and have twelve baskets left over; that's not ordinary Math; that's not even New Math; that's amazing Math! And so you must know more about Math than anyone who has walked this earth.
When your step-dad is a carpenter and you a helpful and loving son, you must know more about Shop than anyone who has walked this earth.

When you can curse a fig tree and cause it to wither and die, you must know more about Botany than anyone who has walked this earth.

When your best friend has been dead for four days and you stand outside his tomb and shout his name and his dead body springs to life, you must know more about Biology, than anyone who has walked this earth.

And when on your last day, you say good-bye to your friends and looking up to Heaven say 'Father I'm coming home'. And when you defy Gravity to join your Father, you must know more about Physics than anyone who has walked this earth.

Yes, Jesus can and will indeed help you throughout high school. All you have to do is ask.

"With this speech, I wanted to demonstrate to the children that if they started everything they did from the inside out, and developed a one-to-one relationship with Jesus, their success would be assured, because he had been through anything they would ever go through, and that he triumphed. I wanted them at an early age, to become aware of the reality of Jesus, and his connection to their lives and their success in life."

What Parents Need To Know

"But there is one other thing we miss," said Tommy.
"What's that?" asked Pierre.
"It is the vital role parents must play in being connected to Jesus themselves as their children must be. They play the singularly most important role in the lives of their children. And not only by providing life's comforts and needs, but most importantly, understanding how their connection to God and their obedience to His commandments are vital to their children's success.
Just as He made a promise to the children, that if they honoured their mother and father He would give them a long and successful life, likewise He has made a promise to the parents. If they obey His commandments, He would bless them as He blessed His children in Old Testament times:
'And if you obey the voice of the Lord your God, being careful to do all his commandments…all these blessings shall come upon you and overtake you, if you obey the voice of the Lord your God.
Blessed shall you be in the city, and blessed shall you be in the field. Blessed shall be the fruit of your body and the fruit of your ground, and the fruit of your beasts, the increase of your cattle, and the young of your flock. Blessed shall be your basket and your kneading-trough. Blessed shall you be when you come in, and blessed shall you be when you go out.' [Deuteronomy 28:1-6]*1*

Parents' obedience to God's word ensures their children's success.
As their children's first teacher, parents need to ensure that they introduce their children to God so that they can learn how to nurture their relationship with Him. They need to teach their children how to live from the inside out".

What Teachers Need To Know

"Just as I wanted children and parents to grasp the importance of Jesus in their lives, I wanted the teachers to grasp the awesome responsibility they have in mentoring children and leading them to Jesus. I tried to do that in another speech I gave at the opening of a new school. In my closing remarks I said:

As we close, I would like to pay a brief tribute to a very special group of people, our teachers. But let me first declare my bias: I am the son of a teacher. That should say it all.

It is my belief that there is no greater vocation, with no greater and enduring responsibility, than teaching.

For us mere mortals, when God calls us to account on the last day, we will be lucky if there is a record of our work. For the teacher, however, it's different. On the last day when God calls your names, for each of you He will have your class lists. And He will go through each name on those lists, and ask: 'What did you do for Maria, for John, for Phillip'. And you will be required to give an account of each student on those lists.

At the end, Jesus will take you by the hand and lead you to a mountain- top. And from that mountain- top, as far as the eye could see, there will be myriads and myriads of people. And you will turn to Jesus and ask: 'Who are these people, Lord?' And he will say to you: 'These are the people you taught'. And you will say to him: 'This can't be Lord'. And he will respond to you: 'Yes, they are. You see, everyone you taught on that list, went on to influence another, and each one of those another – and the number grew exponentially from generation to generation, long after you were gone.'

And in that moment, Jesus will say to you: 'Well done, my good and faithful servant. You did well in little things, I will now put you in charge of bigger things'.

That's why you teach. That's why you're so important. That's why I believe that there is no greater calling than teaching: not medicine, not law, not science. None. Here's why:

Not everyone will need a doctor, but every doctor needs a teacher. Not everyone will need a lawyer, but every lawyer needs a teacher. Even a teacher needs a teacher. That's how important you are, and that's why we treasure you.

So as you follow in the footsteps of the greatest teacher of all time, Jesus; as you take the hands of his little ones and lead them down the narrow road, be careful to be his hands of hope, the channel of his love and kindness, so that on the last day when Jesus takes you by the hand and leads you to that mountain-top, he will indeed be able to turn to you and say: 'Well done my good and faithful servant'.

So thank you for all you do, and may God bless you and keep you as you continue in His service.

After a brief pause, Tommy continued: "If the world only knew the importance of teachers in transforming lives, teachers would be accorded their rightful place atop its social hierarchy. My hope is that people would realize the vital role teachers play and that they would one day be given all the support they need to enhance the lives of the next generations. And I hope that teachers realize the tremendous role that God has given them to lead His children to Him. All of this could be accomplished if we are able to put God at the centre of everything we do."
"That's a tall order though, dad. There are so many distractions pulling us away from the centre, that it is very difficult to remain centred," said Pierre.
"True", replied Tommy, "but if we live a little more consciously in questioning and appreciating the marvelous creation around us, that questioning and appreciation will inevitably lead us back to the centre."
"What do you mean?" Pierre asked.
"If we seek God in His vast creation for example, we will find Him. His other creatures do."

What Our Black Lab Taught Me

"Let me tell you a story about Tammy, our Black Labrador Retriever. When Tammy was a pup I got the job to take her to her first obedience class. I prepared the van by laying the obligatory blanket on the middle seat so that she could lie there while I drove her to her class.
I opened the door of the van and she hopped in and laid on the blanket. This was her first ride in a vehicle. As I drove off, the motion startled her and she stood up on the seat and looked around. Before long she found her way to the front seat beside me. With her nose pressed against the glass, she gazed out the window in amazement. Intrigued by her curiosity, I rolled down the window so that she could get a better view.

She immediately put her front paws on the window sill, pinned back her ears and sniffed at the air racing by her face. Then she did an interesting thing: she began biting the wind. It was as if she was saying: 'What is this thing? I can feel it, I can smell it, yet I can't see it'.

She was experiencing the reality of something she could not see, yet knew to be real.

After her first obedience class we returned to the van. This time she went straight to the front seat and the window. This time she placed her chin on the window sill, pinned back her ears, and with a look of contentment, was as still as a stone as she enjoyed the ride home. It was as if between her trip to obedience school and the end of her class, she had arrived at a deep understanding and acceptance of the reality of the wind. Her unconditional acceptance of that reality stirred in me thoughts of the reality of God.

I have never looked at the wind the same way since. Every time a gentle breeze brushes my face, I remember what our Black Lab taught me: that what is invisible is also real. Invariably, if our heart seeks God, He will find unique ways to reveal Himself to us and lead us to the centre."

"Pierre! Pierre!" called Pierre's mom from inside the house.

"We're out here mom!" Pierre replied.

Pierre's mom opened the front door and peeked out. "Oh, that's where you guys are. Aren't you going to have something to eat?" asked mom.

"What time is it?" asked Tommy.

"It's twelve o'clock," mom replied.

"Already?" Tommy replied in amazement.

The morning had gone by in a flash while he and Pierre were talking. The sun had moved to the centre of the heavens and the shadows of the trees had shortened. But that's typical of conversations between Tommy and his son. When they talk they become so engrossed in conversation that they become suspended in time, oblivious to time and their surroundings.

Mom's talk of food stirred the emptiness in their stomachs and so they followed her to the kitchen where a scrumptious meal awaited.

The three sat down, bowed their heads, blessed and gave thanks for the meal and began eating in silence.

Then mom asked, "What were you guys talking about out there?"

"Oh different things," Pierre replied. "Dad started to tell me about retirement and how he longed to pack things in and relax. Then I asked him what he planned to do with his time and suggested that he could use it to write about some of the conversations we had. Dad didn't think he could write a book, so I gave him some suggestions about the things he could write about; and before long we got into one of our long conversations."

"I see", mom replied.

The remainder of the meal was spent in silence, with Pierre, his mom and Tommy deep in thought. Pierre was thinking about what else he could ask his dad; Tommy was thinking how enjoyable the meal was and Pierre's mom wondering what it would be like having Tommy at home after he retired.

They ended the meal, cleared the table and placed the dishes in the sink.

"Thanks for a great meal mom," said Tommy.

"Yeah, thanks mom," Pierre chimed in. "That was real good.

"You're welcome," mom answered.

"Dad", Pierre began.

"Yes son," answered Tommy.

"Could we go back outside and talk some more?" asked Pierre.

"Sure thing," Tommy replied. "Right after we do the dishes."

After they washed and dried the dishes, Tommy and Pierre went back to the front porch. The porch was now in the shade as the sun had moved further west. The sky was azure blue, and dotted with clouds that looked like giant bales of cotton thrown carelessly about the sky. A peace had settled over the neighbourhood as Pierre and Tommy sat down to resume their conversation.

Chapter 3

Love From The Inside Out

Life And Love

"Could we talk about things like love, success, careers, decision-making, and things like that now dad?"
"Sure," replied Tommy. "To be successful at them all, you must begin at the centre. With love, for example, you start with God, because 'God is love'. First you learn to love Him, then yourself, then your family, then your neighbour."
"I have trouble figuring out how to love God," said Pierre. "I don't know whether love for Him is an emotional thing, a mental thing, or something else. I guess in a way I'm having the same trouble you had when you were growing up. I'm having trouble getting my head around God."
"The fact that you are trying to get your head around Him, shows that you are well on your way to loving Him," Tommy responded.
"Remember though how I got my head around Him. I first got my head around Jesus. I remember asking Jesus one day: 'Lord how can I really love you?' Immediately, the following words sprang to mind: 'If you love me, you will keep my commandments'. [John 14:13]*1*
It's as simple as that. By the way, the way in which those words sprang to my mind, is one of the ways that God speaks to us and advises us. He will quickly bring to mind a verse of scripture, a hymn, a quote from a book, with the answers to questions we might have, or solutions to problems. That's why it's a good practice

to memorize hymns and verses of scripture. They provide the vehicle of communication with God.
By obeying God's commandments then, you lay the foundation for love. When you begin to love God, you then begin to exhibit all the characteristics of love as Paul describes it, when he says in part:

> *Love is patient and kind; love is not Jealous or boastful; it is not arrogant or rude. Love does not insist on its own Way; it is not irritable or resentful; it Does not rejoice at wrong, but rejoices in the right. Love bears all things, believes all things, hopes all things, endures all things. [1 Corinthians 13:4-7]*[2]

When you begin to exhibit these characteristics, you know that you have love: love for family, love for friends, love for that special someone. It's all the same love, from the same source.
But you don't have to worry son, you already show love. And you already show it from the inside out."

A Letter Of Love

"One Fathers' Day, not too long ago, you wrote me a letter of love. Do you remember what you wrote?" asked Tommy.
"No I don't", Pierre replied. "That was some time ago."
"I do", replied Tommy, "because it was one of the greatest presents I ever received. It was for me a badge of honour. Your letter told me not only how much you love me, but also told me that I had finally achieved my goal of being a dad.
I had long wanted to be a dad, but was never sure if I had made it, until that day. You see, being a father is

easy. Anyone can be a father, but it's tough to be a dad; and on that Fathers' Day, when I opened your letter, I knew that I had finally become a dad. On that memorable day you wrote to me:

'Hey Dad,

There isn't much that I can say here that you don't already know. Thank you for being such a huge part of my life. I look around at so many people who do not have any relationship with their fathers, and it makes me even more thankful for the role that you play in my existence.

We talk almost every day. And you've really been blowing my mind at how good you are at this dad stuff. You always tell me that success is when opportunity meets preparation, but you have not had any practice or example of fatherhood.

You do nothing but show me every day how amazing you are and how amazing I will be if I just follow in your footsteps.

I love that. I love you.

I know that I complain a lot and feel lost and alone often; but know that I consider you to be my best friend. You are the only person who has NEVER failed me as a support and guide, and I will spend the rest of my life trying to thank and pay you back in the least.

People always tell me that I'm filled with more energy and passion than they've ever seen. Yet I think of it as nothing, when I compare myself to you.

You make it look soo easy. You're the best. I've got to start taking some notes for myself to use.'

"Wow!" Tommy exclaimed. "That for me was validation beyond anything I had envisioned."

"But it's all true though", Pierre responded.

"And that son is what love is all about. Already you are showing love from the inside out."

A momentary silence descended on Tommy and Pierre; both absorbed in their thoughts, struck by the reality of the bond that existed between them. Until now Tommy was not sure whether he was a dad, let alone a good dad. From the beginning he had struggled to do his best, never sure whether he had measured up.

Pierre's words took him back to his teenage years, where in a fit of despondency he made a promise to himself. He swore then that he would never treat his wife as his father had treated his mother. And never would he treat his children as his father treated him. Some forty years later, he seemed to have kept his promise, or at the very least well on his way to keeping it. The fact that Pierre thought him a good dad was both comforting and satisfying.

He was also comforted by the fact that he was able to let go of the feelings of despondency and resentment of his teenage years; feelings that tend to impede one's internal growth and personal development, and make something of himself.

Not only that, he was able to shake off the challenges of the past and take ownership of his life choices, despite his personal history of growing up without a dad.

Chapter 4

Success From The Inside Out

A Catalyst For Success

The cooing sound of a dove could be heard in the distance. It brought with it a flood of memories for Tommy. The endless days when he would be alone on the farm and the cooing doves would be his only companions.

Back then, as he worked alone he would wonder about the future, dreaming about the day when he would make something of himself. He was never sure what success would look like. All he knew then was that he wanted to be somebody. He remembers as if it were yesterday, the moment he consciously decided to make something of himself.

He was about six years old when a foreign missionary, Fr. Cosgrove came to preach at his church. Fr. Cosgrove's sermon was on the parable of the talents.

...a man going on a journey called his servants and entrusted to them his property; to one he gave five talents, to another two, to another one, to each according to his ability. Then he went away. He who had received the five talents went at once and traded with them; and he made five talents more. So also, he who had the two talents made two talents more. But he who had received the one talent went and dug in the ground and hid his master's money.

Now after a long time the master of those servants came and settled accounts with them. And he who had received the five talents came forward, bringing five talents more, saying, 'Master, you delivered to me five talents; here I have made five talents more.' His master said to him, 'Well done, good and faithful servant; you have been faithful over a little, I will set you over much; enter into the joy of your master.' And he also who had the two talents came forward, saying, 'Master you delivered me two talents; here I have made two talents more.' His master said to him, 'Well done, good and faithful servant; you have been faithful over a little, I will set you over much; enter into the joy of your master.' He also who had received the one talent came forward, saying, 'Master, I knew you to be a hard man, reaping where you did not sow, and gathering where you did not winnow; so I was afraid, and I went and hid your talent in the ground. Here you have what is yours.' But his master answered him, 'You wicked and slothful servant! You knew that I reap where I have not sowed, and gather where I have not winnowed? Then you ought to have invested my money with the bankers, and at my coming I should have received what was my own with interest. So take the talent from him, and give it to him who has the ten talents. For to every one who has will more be given, and he will have abundance; but from him who has not, even what he has will be taken away.' [Matthew 25:14-29][1]

Tommy remembers how dismayed he was at the servant who simply buried his talent and did not put it to good use.
But he was also thrilled to see the rewards that befell those who used their talents wisely, rather than bury them.
He committed on that day, never to waste the talents he had been given. He became driven; not to be rich and famous, but driven to succeed because he wanted to be sure that when the day came for him to give an account of his stewardship, he would be able to stand up and tell

his Master how he had used the talents that He had given him.
"What are you thinking about dad?" asked Pierre.
"I was just thinking about what triggered my drive to succeed," Tommy responded.
"Oh you mean the Fr. Cosgrove sermon that you told me about?"
"Yes", Tommy replied. "It's amazing how certain events can act as powerful catalysts in our lives; but more powerful I think are the influences of those closest to us, and our response to those influences.
As I look back over the years the person who had the most profound and lasting influence on me was my mom. In every respect I am my mother's son. The root of my success though has not only been my mother's influence, but also how I responded to her influence.

Honour Your Father And Your Mother

"I had a deep and profound respect for my mom. I honoured her and obeyed her in all things. I trusted her judgment and advice. I took the direction she gave me, and walked as she directed. Little did I know then that in so honouring her, I was obeying a commandment and laying the foundation for my own success.
Paul in one of his letters refers to that commandment as a commandment with a promise: If you honour mom and dad, not only will you have long life, but you will also have a prosperous life.
"Is this what you attribute to your success?" asked Pierre.
"Absolutely," Tommy replied. "It is one of the foundations of success."
"I remember how struck I was about this fact in reading about Jesus's first miracle – his first major success."
"Which one was that again?" asked Pierre.

"The marriage feast at Cana, where they ran out of wine. Jesus's mom came to him and said: 'They have no wine.' Jesus's first reaction was akin to saying: 'Mom, what does that have to do with us?' But here is the part that really struck me; Mary never argued with Jesus. She simply said to the servants: 'Do whatever he tells you.' [John 2:1-11][2]
Mary knew implicitly that Jesus would do her bidding, because she knew that he honoured her, in keeping with his Father's commandment.
We know of course, how the story ended: Jesus asked the servants to fill the jars with water, and then asked them to draw some. When they drew the water, it had become wine.
This first major success of Jesus's grew out of his habit of honouring his parents.
The most important requirement for success, however, is demonstrated in the story of the rich young man."

The Rich Young Man

"A young man one day asked Jesus: 'Good Teacher, what must I do to inherit eternal life?' Jesus responded: "You know the commandments: 'Do not kill, Do not commit adultery, Do not steal, Do not bear false witness, Do not defraud, Honour your father and mother.'" The young man replied: "Teacher, all these I have observed from my youth." [Mark 10:17-20][3]
Success in the after life as well as the present life relies on the same foundation: obeying God's Commandments; the ones we learned as children:

> [1]."*I am the Lord your God,...*
> *"You shall have no other gods before me.*
> *[2]."You shall not make for yourself a*
> *graven image, or any*

Likeness of anything that is in heaven above, or that is in
the earth beneath, or that is in the water under the earth;
you shall not bow down to them or serve them; for I the
Lord your God am a jealous God, visiting the iniquity of
The fathers upon the children to the third and the fourth
Generation of those who hate me, but showing steadfast
Love to thousands of those who love me and keep my
Commandments.

[3]."You shall not take the name of the Lord your God in vain;
For the Lord will not hold him guiltless who takes his name
In vain.
[4]."Remember the Sabbath day, to keep it holy. Six days you
Shall labour, and do all your work; but the seventh day is a
Sabbath to the Lord your god; in it you shall not do any
Work, you, or your son, or your daughter, your manservant
Or your maidservant, or your cattle, or the sojourner who is
Within your gates; for in six days the Lord made heaven
And earth, the sea, and all that is in them, and rested the

Seventh day; therefore the Lord blessed the Sabbath day
And hallowed it.
[5]."Honour your father and your mother, that your days may
Be long in the land which the Lord your god gives you.
[6]."You shall not kill.
[7]."You shall not commit adultery.
[8]."You shall not steal.
[9]."You shall not bear false witness against your neighbour.
[10]."You shall not covet your neighbour's house; you shall not
covet your neighbour's wife, or his manservant, or his
maidservant, or his ox, or his ass, or anything, that is your
neighbour's." [Deuteronomy 5:6-21][4]

There are several significant things about the young man: he was young, and he was rich. But above all, from his youth, he obeyed all the commandments. It is no surprise therefore, that he was successful at a very young age. He epitomized all that God asks us to do: 'to seek Him first, and He will give us the desires of our heart' – live from the inside out.

Just imagine the success we would have if we simply did as the young man did and obeyed God's commandments; we would be successful beyond our wildest dreams!

So follow the rich young man's example, confident in the knowledge that obedience to God's commandments and your faith in Him, guarantees success. As Jesus said: "Therefore do not be anxious, saying, 'What shall we eat?' or 'What shall we drink?' or 'What shall we wear?' For the Gentiles seek all these things; and your heavenly Father

knows that you need them all. But seek first his kingdom and his righteousness, and all these things shall be yours as well." [Matthew 6:31-33][5]
Live life from the inside out, putting God first, and all things will be granted you.

As I have observed successful people over the years, I have always been struck by how much the truly successful ones honour their parents.
The world's greatest athletes in golf, basketball and hockey all exhibit a deep love and respect for their parents.
Because these athletes honour their parents, God keeps the promise made in His commandment, by multiplying their successes.
Children who honour their parents find success with ease. Those who don't, struggle to find success".
"If keeping God's commandments is the cornerstone of success, what else contributes to success?" asked Pierre.

Practice, Practice, Practice

"I think it's important to understand that success in anything we do requires practice. The athletes I alluded to earlier, all are tremendously talented. Yet during their careers, few if any of their peers practiced as long and as hard as they did. They generally arrived at practice first, and stayed long after everyone else had left.
It is in those lonely moments of practice and reflection that you hone your skills and think of new and unique ways of doing things, and doing them well. Not only that, the things you practice today, prepare you for future success.
Take David, for example; he spent a lot of lonely hours, days and nights practicing to use his sling shot with deftness and skill. He practiced on wild animals, keeping them away from destroying his father's sheep. Little did he

know that such practice would be a stepping stone to becoming king of Israel.
Because of his skill with the sling shot, he was able to defeat Goliath, and eventually ascend to the throne.
Without practice, therefore, you cannot achieve true success.
Take the simple act of walking, for example; the only reason you can walk is because you practice walking everyday. If you were to simply stop walking, your muscles would atrophy and become useless. Practice is therefore critical to success. Practice alone won't do it though. You must also learn to do more than the bare minimum."

Do More Than The Bare Minimum

"You cannot simply do only what's required and expect to achieve a high level of success. If the student, for example, merely does what is assigned, and does no research beyond the work given, that student will not truly succeed.
If the worker merely does what is assigned, she will not truly succeed. In doing more than the bare minimum in all of your endeavours, you build capacity to succeed. You expand your horizons and so out-perform those who are content with just doing what's required of them.
By stretching yourself, you in fact do what we are all called to do, namely: to constantly grow beyond our current state."
After a brief moment of silence a smile spread over Pierre's face.
"What is it?" asked Tommy.
"I don't know why I thought about this", Pierre chuckled, "But you said something to me once that I thought was funny, yet I will never forget. I was complaining about something and I remember you saying to me: 'Well Pierre, what you need to do more of is to look, listen and shut your mouth'. Is that important for success?" Pierre asked.

Look, Listen And Be Quiet

"I believe so", responded Tommy. I think God gave us two eyes, two ears and one mouth for a reason. I believe He expects us to actively listen more, observe more and talk less.

If you live by this rule, you will find that you are able to absorb more information and as a result learn more. And the more knowledge you have, the greater your chances of success. When you are a good observer and a good listener, you become a very active participant in the world around you and are able to see and find opportunities in the world that others miss.

My mom had a very unique way of teaching us how to be good observers of the world. She would often give us "pop quizzes" about local events, world events or sometimes, seemingly unimportant events. One incident in particular stands out in my mind.

One Sunday morning my mom, my siblings and I were walking to church. As we passed the local shop I noticed a brand new sign attached to the shop. It must have been put up the day before, because I was seeing it for the first time. The sign was an advertisement by the Coca Cola ® Company, announcing their newest product called Fanta®. In bold letters the sign read: 'Fantastically Flavourful'.

The moment I saw the sign, the first thought that entered my mind was: 'mom is going to ask us about the sign.' On our return from church, as we approached the shop, I hung back from everyone, stopped at the sign, and memorized the spelling of the words. I then ran to catch up with the others and we continued on our way home.

We had barely entered the door when my mom turned to my sister and said: 'Brandy, spell fantastically'. My sister was stumped. Mom then turned to me and said:

'Tommy, spell fantastically'. Without missing a beat I responded 'f-a-n-t-a-s-t-i-c-a-l-l-y.' 'Now spell flavourful'. Again I responded: 'f-l-a-v-o-u-r-f-u-l.' Mom nodded her satisfaction and we all changed from our Sunday best, and went about our business for the day.

That ability to observe and listen has stayed with me since. It has on occasion allowed me to see more than others see, and to grasp more than others do; to look for and find opportunities for success, where others see and find none. The power and effectiveness of that skill came home to me when I worked at the General Hospital."

"I remember you telling me that story once. What happened there again?" Pierre asked.

Look For And Find Opportunities For Success

"When I first arrived in Canada, like nearly all new immigrants I had trouble finding work. After a long, frustrating and demoralizing search, I eventually landed a temporary position as a floor cleaner at the hospital. On my first day of work I donned my grey uniform, was handed my broom, bucket and mop, and began my career in Canada as a floor cleaner. I set out to be the best floor cleaner I could be. I would sweep my assigned area, then mop it. Then I would wash the sinks and toilets, clean the mirrors. I made sure that everywhere and everything sparkled. All the while I worked I would be humming or singing a tune. I remember one day in particular, as I was scrubbing the bathroom and singing away, the door opened and a nurse poked her head in and said: 'Oh it's you in there. I was wondering who could be so happy cleaning toilets'. She then closed the door and left.

Before long, word got around about this new floor cleaner with a good attitude.
As the weeks went by I grew anxious, because my temporary position would be coming to an end. One day during a break in my shift, I sat at a table in the cafeteria with some men wearing white uniforms. In the course of our conversation I asked them what they did. They said they were Orderlies. I then asked what an Orderly did. They explained to me that they cared for male patients. They were responsible for feeding them, cleaning them and giving them non-medical care as needed.
I returned to my shift that evening and decided that I would apply for an Orderly's position the next day. Not only would the job be permanent, but it was also offered in various shifts, a situation that would allow me the flexibility of going to school at night.
When the next day came, before the start of my shift, I visited the human resources office and told Mr. Howman that I would like to apply for an Orderly's position. Not surprisingly, Mr. Howman indicated that there were no Orderly positions available, but that if a permanent floor cleaning job came up, he would let me know. I thanked him for his time and left.
During my conversations with the Orderlies I had learned that the head of the Orderlies was a Mr. McMahon. So no sooner had I left the human resources office when I sought out Mr. McMahon's office and knocked on his door. He looked up, and to my surprise said, 'Come in Tommy'. I then told him my plight, and told him that I would like a job as an Orderly. 'Not a problem,' he said. ' I have heard a lot of good things about you.'
When my cleaning assignment was finished, I joined Mr. McMahon's team. After a brief training period, I donned my white uniform, began earning a little more

money, and an equal measure of respectability. In time I learned to enjoy this sometimes challenging, sometimes messy job.

One day I was asked to relieve one of my colleagues in the Recovery Room. The Recovery Room was the place where patients who had just had surgery were taken to recover from the operation before being taken to their rooms. My job was to wheel patients from the Operating Room to the Recovery Room and eventually to their respective floors.

On the day in question, as I was sitting in the adjoining room waiting to wheel the next patient to the Recovery Room, Dr. McSween, the head of Gynecology walked in. He said 'hello', and asked who I was and where I was from. His eyes lit up when I told him the name of my homeland, as he had sailed that area many times. He wanted to know why I would leave 'Paradise' to endure such cold winters. I told him I had come to attend university, and hoped to return home some day.

When it was time for the patient to be wheeled into the Recovery Room, I excused myself and went to get the patient. I donned my mask and gown, went into the Operating Room and waited while the Anesthetist brought the patient to consciousness.

While I waited, I was observing the different people present, as well as the proceedings. After I wheeled the patient into the Recovery Room, I went back to the adjoining room. Dr. McSween was still there, as his patient had not yet arrived. I sat down and asked him about the people in the operating Room and the roles that they played. As I identified each one by what they were wearing and doing, he explained which ones were nurses, doctors and surgical assistants.

The role of surgical assistant intrigued me, so I asked him: 'What does a surgical assistant do?' He explained that they assisted the surgeon by handing her/him the instruments needed to perform the operation in question. I then asked: 'what qualifications are required to be a S/A?' He responded that no particular qualifications were necessary, just training in the use of instruments, operating room procedures and sterilization procedures. I then surprised him with my next question: 'Could I be a Surgical Assistant?' He thought for a moment then replied: 'Usually these positions are reserved for medical students during the summer, but let me think about it.'

A few days went by. When I next saw Dr. McSween he said to me 'Oh by the way Tommy, I had a chance to speak with the nurses with whom you work. They all spoke very highly of you. So I tell you what, next summer you will be a Surgical Assistant.'

When summer came, I joined a group of medical students. We learned the names of instruments, how to sterilize instruments, operating room procedures and the method of handing instruments to surgeons during operations.

That summer I had the experience of a lifetime. I assisted in operations ranging from face lifts to kidney biopsies; all because I looked for and found opportunities for success right where I worked."

"Wow!" exclaimed Pierre. "Was moving from floor cleaner to Surgical Assistant that easy?" he asked.

"It was made easy because I was an excellent floor cleaner, with a good attitude," Tommy replied. "Not only that, I was willing to take a menial job and not feel demeaned by it; it was honest work that I did with pride and with a willing spirit. I showed curiosity. I asked questions to get information, and acted on the information.

I didn't take 'no' for an answer when Mr. Howman turned down my request for a better job. I persevered

and used discretion in finding a way other than through Mr. Howman.
I took the risk of attempting something completely new, and for which I had no initial training. That willingness to take risk provided me with an enriching and rewarding experience. And that wonderful experience was as a result of my commitment to excellence in all things great or small.
Nothing beats excellence. Nothing beats a habit of doing all things well." Tommy continued.

Do All Things Well

"Excellence has a way of becoming your spokesperson. Even in situations where people attempt to put obstacles in your way, by doing excellent work you are able to speak above their heads, to those with the power to clear away road blocks and to facilitate success."
"I get the sense that excellence is this grand statement; an elaborate expression of a job well done. Is that the case?" asked Pierre.
"It could be," replied Tommy. "But even if it finds expression in big things, it has its genesis in the practice of doing little things well."
"What do you mean?" asked Pierre.
"You know how I ask you guys to wash the dishes, make your beds, and tidy your rooms?"
"Yes," Pierre replied.
"And you know how I get after you if it's not done well?"
"Yes," Pierre responded.
"Well, these chores have as much to do with being helpful, as with helping you cultivate a habit of excellence in small things. If you do small things well, that habit automatically spills over when you do big

things. However, if you only do things well some of the time, you end up living life by exception."
"What do you mean?" Pierre asked.

Avoid Living By Exception

"Living by exception means only doing things well when you feel like it; turning excellence on and off as it suits you."
"Is there a danger in that?" asked Pierre.
"Certainly," Tommy replied. "The danger is, on the day in which you really need to turn it on, you might not be able to muster the will or the frame of mind to do so, thereby causing your performance to fall flat in critical situations. This malady of living by exception exists at both the individual level as well as the team level. Successful sports teams, for example, are the ones that are always 'up' for every game, no matter the opponent. Unsuccessful teams on the other hand, are the ones that are 'up' only when they play the good teams. More often than not, they fall flat even against poorer teams, because they are unable to rise to the occasion when it is critical for them to do so.
By practicing to do all things well, therefore, you develop a high- performance habit. You cultivate a power within that requires no external stimulus to drive it. When you develop that fire within, you do not need anyone to motivate you to do excellent work. You do not need to be an eye servant."

Do Not Be An Eye Servant

"If you need external approval to do excellent work, you are merely an eye servant."
"What's an eye servant?" asked Pierre.

"An eye servant is someone who only does good work when someone is looking at them. The moment no one is looking, they revert to performing poorly or not at all," said Tommy.

"How could I avoid being an eye servant?" Pierre asked.

"Try to find joy and contentment in your work. Also understand that everything you do prepares you for the next phase of your development as a human being. No matter how insignificant it might seem; how mundane. Everything you do is always a life lesson to prepare you for what's to come.

Sometimes people complain about being unsuccessful, but miss this simple lesson. They believe that success comes with doing big things. Truth is, success begins with doing little things, and doing them well.

The other thing to remember is this: everything we need to succeed is given to us every day. It could be as simple as something a friend says, or advice given by a parent or teacher, the words from a song, a tragedy. People who succeed are open to their surroundings, and so are able to see opportunities and act on them.

Those who don't succeed live life on automatic pilot and are closed to their surroundings, thereby failing to see and to take advantage of the lessons being offered. They may on occasion recognize the lessons being taught, but fail to act; and action is a fundamental requirement for success. Some people don't act on things because they are afraid to fail. Yet even when you fail, failure should not be seen as something negative."

Failure Is An Option

"Truth is, failure is merely the flip side of the success coin. It is of the same currency. If we learn from failure,

that learning yields wisdom. Through wisdom we make better decisions which in turn enable success.
It can be a wonderful thing failure; as long as you learn from its lessons. We cannot escape it; it is an integral part of life. Once you accept that fact, it frees you to both try and achieve extraordinary things. It adds buoyancy to life and creates the boundaries that temper and guide success. It creates opportunities for learning; invitations to grow beyond our present state.
Failure, you see, is an exceptional teacher. She never lets you down. If there is a lesson you can't master, she keeps repeating it until you learn.
Your chance of failure will be substantially minimized, however, if you focus on the present."

Take Care Of Today – Tomorrow Will Take Care Of Itself

"It is important for us to remain grounded in 'today' and understand the importance of 'today' in our lives. We can do nothing about yesterday, except to learn from it and use it as prologue for today.
We can do everything possible today, to ensure a better tomorrow.
If you do the very best you can today, follow all the success characteristics we have been talking about, success will overtake you today and tomorrow. Action today, is what will propel you to success tomorrow."

Life Is Like An Automatic Door

"Life is like an automatic door. If you simply stand before it and do nothing, nothing happens. The moment you step toward it, however, it opens up itself to reveal incredible opportunities. And as long as you keep walking and exploring, it keeps opening, leading you to success beyond your wildest dreams.

But in order to partake of life's treasures you must be conscious of what it offers, and be open and willing to participate."

Live Life With A Willing Spirit

"In addition to living with an awareness of what life has to offer, you should also cultivate and live with a willing and helpful spirit.

Look for ways to help out at home, at school, at work; wherever you are. That willingness to help not only brings joy to others, but also brings untold blessings to you. It also develops a habit of helpfulness in you that will never let you down or betray you.

My mom once told me a carpenter's story: There was a carpenter who worked for his boss for over thirty years. Finally, he was due to retire. The day before he was to retire, his boss said to him: 'Johnny there is one more job I want you to do before you leave. There is a house on the south lot I would like you to finish for me.'

This made Johnny angry. He knew the detail and time that would be needed to do the work, and he certainly couldn't finish it before his retirement date.

Johnny went down to the house anyway and started the work his boss had asked him to do. Johnny's anger got the better of him. In stead of the excellent, painstaking work he normally did, Johnny did a slipshod job, using inferior materials, and hastily put things together.

The house looked lousy. Johnny finished the job and went back to his boss to let him know. After he told his boss he was finished, his boss opened his desk drawer and handed a set of keys to Johnny saying: 'Johnny, here are the keys to the house. This is my retirement gift to you.' Johnny's jaw dropped as he stammered: 'but, but, why didn't you tell me it was mine; if I had known it was mine I would have done a better job.'
When we are not consistently helpful, or willing, or excellent, in the end we let ourselves down and become the ultimate losers. The lesson is not merely about doing things, but also about doing them well from start to finish."

Finish Everything You Start

"When we fail to finish what we start, we miss a critical building block of success. Since each stage of our development builds on the previous stage, if we do not complete the earlier stages, we leave gaps in our learning.
Those gaps are widened and compounded with each succeeding stage, setting us up for failure, or at best, limited success.
So when we are called upon to do things, no matter how boring, mundane or insignificant, we are called upon because there is a lesson or lessons to be learned. It could be we need to learn discipline, build character, or any number of life skills. The key is to do them well, do them with a willing spirit, and finish them. Because unfinished works are life lessons missed."

The Power Of Education

"Education is another critical building block of success. I learned this long ago from my mom. Mom had this incredible ability to illustrate a point in the most powerful and poignant way. I remember as if it were yesterday, a lesson she gave us, following a vicious and destructive hurricane. In the aftermath of the storm, mom took my siblings and me around the farm to survey the damage. Slowly and carefully mom walked through the land with her children in tow. The air was pungent with the smell of tree sap and spices. Trees with shattered and bleeding limbs hung their heads, exhausted from the battering they had endured the night before.

There was a sense of everything having been washed clean. Grass lay matted and smooth in some places, like the long locks of a giant mermaid, brushed into place by the storm's rushing waters.

There was an eerie stillness in the air, interrupted occasionally by snapping branches underfoot, or the distant wailing of a neighbor over her lost son, swept away from her grasp by the raging torrents of the nearby river, nevermore to be seen.

Not a word was spoken. We simply followed where mom led, doing as she did. After we finished the survey of the destroyed property, mom gathered us around her, and looking at us intently she said in a somber voice: 'You see how easy it is for the things we cultivated to be destroyed. I want you all to cultivate your minds.' Although we were young, there was no need for an explanation. We got the message. That was vintage mom. Such was her ability to use the moment to teach, to drive a point home; and the point did hit home.

For me in particular it was most telling. It set me on a relentless pursuit of knowledge; finding every opportunity to learn, to cultivate my mind.

Knowledge is powerful. It is lightweight and portable. No one can take it from you once you have acquired it. Once you have it employers and others desire it. They fight to get you to work for them, to get you to share your knowledge with them. It endears others to you. That's why school is so important. Since attendance at school is dictated as a requirement to function in the world, and since you live as a member of it, it makes sense to develop the skills and tools that are necessary to succeed in the world. So take school seriously:

- *Fulfill the requirements for each grade level – avoid gaps in education, be the best you can be at each level*
- *Develop a facility in as many subjects as possible – plant as many seeds as you can, as you never know which ones will grow and bear fruit later in life*
- *Since the highest levels of education yield the highest rewards, reach for the highest level of education you possibly can*
- *Be a life-long learner, always upgrading your skills and seeking new knowledge*
- *Share what you know with others. The more you share the more you know. It is an invigorating and enriching cycle"*

Recognizing that he had been speaking at length, Tommy paused for a while and looked at Pierre to see how he was holding up. Pierre looked at him and smiled and Tommy asked: "You holding up alright?"
"Yeah, I am," Pierre replied. "Like all the other times we talk, this means so much to me, and I'm so thankful that you take the time."
"Not a problem", Tommy replied as he playfully ruffled Pierre's hair.
"You know," continued Tommy, "one of the many things I admire about you is your sense of gratitude. This deep sense of gratitude in my view is one of the simplest yet most potent elements of success."

The Power Of Thanks

"There was a young girl called Emily. One day during her math class, she had a very enjoyable and extremely enlightening learning experience. For the first time she fully understood what was taught and felt a great sense of accomplishment.

She was so delighted, that after the class she went up to her teacher and said: 'Miss that was a great class today. You explained things very well. Thank you.'

'Why, thank you Emily, that's very nice of you,' the teacher replied.

As the teacher gathered her books and papers she felt a deep sense of satisfaction. Never before had a student expressed appreciation for what she taught them. Emily's words of thanks made her day.

As the teacher entered the teacher's lounge with a spring in her step and a glow on her face, the first words out of her mouth to her colleagues were: 'The nicest thing happened to me today.' As the other teachers looked up, she continued: 'You know young Emily, the one who is new to our school; after class today she came up to me and thanked me for putting on a wonderful class.'

'I'm not surprised,' one of the teachers replied. 'This young lady shows a lot of class.'

Now there was no ulterior motive in Emily's gesture. That's the way she was raised.

The results of that simple gesture were truly amazing. Not only did Emily's math teacher make sure she understood all the lessons, but the other teachers also looked after Emily. There was no shortage of help when she needed it. Needless to say, Emily had a very successful time at school. Her grades shot up. She made the principal's honour roll and became president of the students' council. A simple word of 'thanks' drove Emily's success.

Jesus showed how important 'thanks' was to him. After he had healed ten lepers, only one of them returned to say 'thanks.' Somewhat disappointed, Jesus asked the man: "Were not ten cleansed? Where are the nine?" He then sent the man home, clearly disappointed that the other nine did not show any gratitude toward him for healing them. [Luke 17:11-19]

God expects us to be thankful for the many blessings he gives us. He expects us to live with an attitude of gratitude. When we fail to thank Him, we behave like the man invited to a rich man's house. The rich man sent a chauffeured limousine to pick up this stranger. When the limousine arrived, the chauffeur opened the door and the man got in without so much as a greeting. Upon arrival at the rich man's house, the butler opened the door and showed the man to his room.

The man partook of all that was given him, never uttering a word of thanks or showing any sense of appreciation. At the end of his stay he simply picked up his bag, walked through the door and went on his way. The rich man and his household were aghast at such boorish behaviour. But that's how we behave, if while living on this earth, we partake of all that God has given us, and not say so much as a 'thank you' to Him.

So saying 'thanks' is critical to success as are other forms of courtesy."

Courtesy

"Courtesy bridges gaps, it disarms, it astounds."

"Do you remember that subway incident you once told me about?" Tommy asked.

"Which one?" asked Pierre.

"The one involving that elderly couple," Tommy replied. "You were on your way home from school and this older couple boarded the crowded subway car. You looked up from your video game and seeing them, you immediately got up and offered the lady your seat. Do you remember their reaction?"

"Yeah, I'll never forget it. It was weird; it was as if they didn't expect that kind of treatment and were totally amazed that I would offer my seat," said Pierre.

"On that day," Tommy continued, "you did more to bridge the age gap and the race gap than any Royal Commission on race and aging could. That's what courtesy does: at work, at play, at school, in society. It fosters relationships and endears people to one another. Those who demonstrate it consistently, invariable draw others to them and find others to be willing and interested parties in their success.

That's what you awakened in that couple. They wanted to know more about you; what you did, what you were studying at university. A simple gesture of courtesy disarmed them and reminded them of a chivalrous time they thought was long lost. You made their day; and I'm sure they went on to make someone else's day as a result of this gesture.

Courtesy; simple words like 'please' and 'thank you'. Simple gestures like offering a seat or opening a door or saying 'hello', are cornerstones of success and the visible demonstration of good character."

Character

"I remember as a child there was a poem we used to recite. I cannot remember it all now, but I remember the first three lines that have stuck with me from childhood to adulthood:

Speak the truth
And speak it ever
Cost it what it will

Truth and honesty were the cornerstones of our character building. Mom raised us to do the right thing no matter what. So for us integrity was not a sliding scale as some would now have you believe. Nor is it a slave to expediency. It is that indelible mark of character by which people must know you, and by which they could trust you unequivocally. That's why it must be taught while young in order for it to be lasting. Just as a tree has to be shaped while it's young, so too must youngsters be shaped."

"What do you mean?" asked Pierre, after being silent for a while.

"Well," explained Tommy, "if you want a tree to grow straight, the best time to guide it is while it is still young and can still be guided. It is supple and flexible then. So all you have to do is put it in the position you would like it to grow, then put a straight stake beside it to guide it. And as night follows day, it will grow as guided by the stake.

If you wait till the tree is grown and try to shape it then, it will be too late. It will have grown according to its own leanings and become too rigid, too inflexible to be shaped and guided.

So too character. While children are still young, you shape them both by precept and example as they should grow: straight, disciplined, honest and with integrity. As a child growing up, my mom was my model. As I grew into adulthood, Jesus became my model."

Chapter 5

Jesus As Model

Jesus is our model for life. When he says: "I am the way the truth and the life," he is inviting us to follow his example; to live life as he did, to find success as he did. He provided the blueprint, clearly defined, through precept and example. Therefore following Jesus is not separate from life. It is life. Every example he has given us we can and must use in everyday living; from our waking moments to when we turn in for the night.

He Loved Honoured And Obeyed His Father

Jesus is the perfect model for life. He showed us how in word and deed and encouraged us to follow his example. He loved his father dearly; he obeyed His Commandments.

> If you keep my commandments, you will abide in
> my love,
> Just as I have kept my father's commandments and
> abide in
> his love. [John 15:10][1]

He Studied The Word

Jesus demonstrated that he studied the word of God throughout his life. His performance at age twelve in the temple with the learned men showed his astounding knowledge and understanding of the word.
Also, when a Pharisee asked him: "Teacher, which is the great commandment in the law?" And he said to him, 'You shall love the Lord your God with all your heart, and with all your soul, and with all your mind.'" [Matthew 22:36-37][2]

When Jesus spoke these words to the Pharisee, he was repeating the very words Moses said to the people of Israel in Old Testament times: "Hear, O Israel: The Lord our God is one Lord; and you shall love the Lord your God with all your heart, and with all your soul, and with all your might." [Deuteronomy 6:4-5][3]
Again, when Jesus was tempted in the desert and said: "It is written, 'man does not live by bread alone, but by every word that proceeds from the mouth of God'" [Matthew 4:4][4] He was again repeating the words that he had studied. Words given by Moses to the people of Israel: "And he humbled you and let you hunger and fed you with manna, which you did not know, nor did your fathers know; that he might make you know that man does not live by bread alone, but that man lives by everything that proceeds out of the mouth of the Lord." [Deuteronomy 8:3][5]

He Prayed Often

'And in the morning, a great while before day, he rose And went out to a lonely place, and there he prayed'. [Mark 1:35][6]
Jesus began his day with God. He began his day from the inside out. Before he did anything he first prayed to his Father. We should also pray to his Father as he did; both morning and evening.
Our morning and evening prayers should act as bookends to days that catalogue the exceptional behaviour we must exhibit toward God, family, neighbours, classmates, colleagues. They should act as supports for our strategies in dealing with challenges and tragedies; all of which must be dealt with from the inside out.
I now understand why mom roused us early in the morning to pray before daybreak, and why she closed

the day with prayer. She was following Jesus's example.

He Prayed For Others

In offering prayers on his disciples' behalf he said: "I am praying for them; I am not praying for the world but for those whom thou hast given me, for they are thine; all mine are thine, and thine are mine, and I am glorified in them." [John 17:9-10][7]

He Gave Thanks In Prayer

"I thank thee Father, Lord of heaven and earth, that thou hast hidden these things from the wise and understanding and revealed them to babes;" [Luke 10:21][8]
"And as they were eating, he took bread, and blessed, and broke it and gave it to them and said, 'Take; this is my body.' And he took a cup, and when he had given thanks he gave it to them and they all drank of it." [Mark 14:22-23][9]

He Prayed When Anguished

"And being in an agony he prayed more earnestly; and his sweat became like great drops of blood falling down upon the ground." [Luke 22:44][10]

He Invited Us To Pray For Our Needs

"Whatever you ask in my name, I will do it…" [John 14:13][11]
The power of prayer is unmistakable. It is most critical in sustaining us and bringing us untold blessings.

He Forgave Those Who Wronged Him – He Bore No Grudges

Even in his last and most anguished moment, he was able to forgive those who had scourged, taunted and crucified him: "Father, forgive them; for they know not what they do." [Luke 23:34][12]
When one of his best friends denied him three times, he held no grudges against him. He demonstrated this by making Peter head of the disciples.

He Loved His Neighbour

He healed those who were sick, fed those who were hungry and offered immense gestures of love to all who asked and came within his sphere of influence.

He Was A Curious Learner

Jesus studied hard. He learned his lessons well. His engaging discussions at age twelve with learned men provide an excellent example of this:

After three days they found him in the temple, sitting among the teachers, listening to them and asking them questions; and all who heard him were amazed at his understanding and his answers. [Luke 3:46-47][13]

He Was An Orator

He was skilled in language arts. His sermon on the mount remains a masterpiece of oratory:

Seeing the crowds, he went up on the mountain, and when he sat down his disciples came to him. And he opened his mouth and taught them saying:

"Blessed are the poor in spirit, for theirs is the kingdom of heaven.
"Blessed are those who mourn, for they shall be comforted.
"Blessed are the meek, for they shall inherit the earth.
"Blessed are those who hunger and thirst for righteousness, for they shall be satisfied.
"Blessed are the merciful, for they shall obtain mercy.
"Blessed are the pure of heart, for they shall see God.
"Blessed are the peacemakers, for they shall be called sons of god.
"Blessed are those who are persecuted for righteousness' sake, for theirs is the kingdom of heaven.
"Blessed are you when men revile you and persecute you and utter all kinds of evil against you falsely on my account. Rejoice and be glad, for your reward is great in heaven, for so men persecuted the prophets who were before you. [Matthew 5:1-12][14]

Through his example, Jesus taught us the importance of good communication. My mom followed Jesus's example and taught us the art of communication.
When I was young, she would use every opportunity to teach me communication and oratory. She employed many strategies, but two stand out for me.
Like her pop quizzes, she would have us make impromptu speeches when we least expected it. After a meal, for example, she would call on one of us to say something about the meal and give a vote of thanks. Of course we never knew which one of us would be called upon, and as a result we had to learn how to think on our feet when we were called to speak.
The other strategy, she used on me in particular. Every now and then, during recess at elementary school, she would send one of her students to get me away from a game of cricket. When that call came I always knew

what it meant: I would be required to do some form of recitation, but never knew what.

With her students out of the class and at recess, mom would sit at the front and send me to the back of the empty school house and would ask me to recite a poem or a quotation of some sort. I had to project my voice, articulate my words and speak as clearly and eloquently as a ten year old could.

In the beginning it would be mom and I alone in the school house. Before long word spread among the students that when Teacher B called Tommy during recess, it was for him to recite or speak about something.

So no sooner was I called in later days, when students would now ring the entire school house, looking through the open windows and watching and listening to me being put through my paces. So now, not only did I have to give an impromptu speech, I now had to do it with an audience.

It was both scary and nerve racking, but it taught me an incredible and important communication skill.

He Showed Deference To Authority

Jesus was in the world, but not of the world; and while in the world he made sure that he observed those things that are necessary for the functioning of civil society. Nowhere is made clear than his attitude toward taxes, when the Pharisees tested him:

"Teacher, we know that you are true, and teach the way of god truthfully, and care for no man; for you do not regard the position of men. Tell us, then, what you think. Is it lawful to pay taxes to Caesar or not?"

And Jesus said to them, after they had shown him a coin with Caesar's likeness: "Render therefore to

Caesar the things that are Caesar's, and to God the things that are God's." [Matthew 22:16-21][15]

Excellence Was His Hallmark

Whatever Jesus undertook, he did it with excellence and with a willing spirit.
One day, after healing a man who was deaf and mute, the people were astonished at what he had done and couldn't withhold their praise for his work, although he commanded them to tell no one:

"And he charged them to tell no one; but the more he charged them, the more zealously they proclaimed it. And they were astonished beyond measure saying, 'He has done all things well; he even makes the deaf hear and the dumb speak.'" [Mark 7:36-37][16]

He Was Multi-Talented

Jesus was multi-talented and used all his talents to the benefit of others. Not only did he work astounding miracles, he also did mundane things like cooking. His specialty being fish and bread which he served to his disciples:

When they got out on land, they saw a charcoal fire there, with fish lying on it and bread.
Jesus said to them, "Come and have breakfast." [John 21:9-12][17]

No one embodied success better than Jesus. You remember how I said earlier that honouring your parents is critical to success? Well it is no coincidence or surprise that Jesus's first major success, his first

miracle, was done by honouring his mother's request: 'Son, they have no wine.'
When you honour your parents, God keeps His promise to you namely: bringing you a long and successful life. And that promise does not end with your parents' passing. It lasts a lifetime.
Now Jesus's life on earth was of course short for a reason. But there is no denying his success. He made the blind to see, the lame walk, the dead he raised to life. So much so, that although many people hated him and wanted him dead, they could not deny an unmistakable fact: that he did all things well. He embodied all and more of the attributes of success we talked about earlier. So if we use him as a model, we will never go wrong, for he is indeed 'the way, the truth and the life.'
If we follow his example our success will be guaranteed.
He will show us how to achieve unqualified success in our lives, our relationships, our careers."
Pierre knitted his brow and had a quizzical look on his face. "What is it Pierre?" asked Tommy.
"I am a little confused," Pierre replied.
"About what?" asked Tommy.
"Well, I'm trying to make sense of what you are telling me; to connect Jesus's work and what he did with my own life. He worked miracles and stuff; but I'm just an ordinary human being, how do I make real the things he did in his time to the things I do in mine? How do I, for example, incorporate what he did in his life into mine? He knew his purpose because his Dad told him and sent him specifically to fulfill it. He knew his Dad. I don't know his Dad and don't know how to even begin to find my purpose and to be useful in life.
So that's what confuses me. All our lives we have been taught to figure out what we want to do in life. Now,

however, you seem to be saying that we really don't have to figure things out," Pierre continued.

"That's right," Tommy responded.

"But wouldn't life then be an aimless, frustrating search if you don't have goals in mind?"

"Only if you think you have to figure it out," Tommy continued. "Let me explain. You remember earlier Jesus said to his disciples: "Therefore I tell you, do not be anxious about your life, what you shall eat, nor about your body, what you shall put on." [Luke 12:22:23]*18*

"Yes," said Pierre.

"Well," said Tommy, "here is what he is exhorting us to do: he wants us to come to grips with the fact that we are God's workmanship, that God has already determined His plans for us, and there is really no need to fret about our purpose in life. Once you accept these facts, all you have to do is agree with God that you simply want to do whatever He has planned for you. With this commitment, you then use His commandments as your guide, and His word as sustenance for the journey."

"I still don't get it," Pierre continued. "Let's say I'm starting out in life, how am I supposed to live? What job am I supposed to have? How do I find direction in what I must do?"

"Aah," said Tommy, "that's where faith comes in."

"Yeah, but, but…," stammered Pierre.

Tommy realizing that frustration was setting in said to Pierre: "Let me help you connect the dots. Remember what we talked about earlier, always deal with things from the inside out; starting always with God? You must therefore begin your life's journey by committing your life to the work He has chosen for you. In so doing, you abandon your quest to fulfill your own desires, and abandon yourself to His will. Once you do that, you let go for God to do His part in the process,

and you to do your part."
"How do I do my part then?" Pierre asked.
"Since you are in the world, you must develop the skills to function in the world. Society requires you to go to school – so go to school; learn what you are required to learn, working hard, and fulfilling all the requirements at every grade level and beyond, as far as you wish to go.
Make a difference at home, in your community; avail yourself of all that's afforded you to function in society. All the while you do your part, keep in constant touch with God as Jesus did, and not only will God lead you to His purpose for you, but He will also give you all the worldly things you desire, just as He did for the rich young man."
"That sounds pretty scary to me," said Pierre. "It's like being a trapeze artist without a safety net."
"It's scary only because from childhood we are taught to take control of our lives and determine for ourselves the purpose we are meant to fulfill on this earth. What I'm telling you contradicts this approach; I am telling you to let go and let God; to walk by faith and not by sight.
There is one unmistakable fact you must come to grips with; it is this: Not one of us had a say in being placed on this earth. God made that determination. There is no way we should therefore beat up ourselves to try to figure out our purpose in life. And there is no way we should try to figure it out without the help of the One who put us here in the first place.
Like I said to the grade eight class, God in His wisdom thought you important enough, good enough, smart enough, to give you a place on this earth. Why would you then doubt your own capabilities when your creator has endowed you with all that you need in life and has confidence in your ability to succeed? It would

therefore be shortsighted of us not to involve Him in the discovery process. We should also be heartened by the fact that God consistently grants success to those who don't have confidence in their own abilities, and who are of humble beginnings. He continues to do this today, just as He did in Old Testament times.

Moses didn't think he was good enough to lead Israel, yet God made him leader. Gideon didn't think was worthy of leading Israel, yet God made him a leader. Saul didn't think he was good enough, yet God made him king of Israel. Ruth rose from humble beginnings to become the mother of Obed, the father of Jesse, the father of David, the father of Solomon. David was a mere keeper of sheep, yet he too rose to be king of Israel.

God knows what's best for us even when we don't always know or don't always think we are good enough. That's why we should always consult Him for guidance as we seek to discover His purpose for our lives."

Tommy paused for a while then asked: "If Jesus were in your position, what would be the first thing he would do?"

"Talk to his Dad?" asked Pierre.

"Exactly," Tommy responded. "He would talk to his Dad in prayer, to seek His help and guidance. And once he has asked, he would leave it up to his Dad to guide him."

"And what do you think Jesus's next step might be?" Tommy continued.

"He would likely look to himself to see what he could do, right where he was, in order to make things happen." Pierre replied.

"What would likely be his next step?" asked Tommy.

"Maybe talk to his parents and seek their advice?"

"Right again," Tommy replied. "He would work from the "inside out". First his Dad, then taking responsibility for his part in the process, then seeking help from those closest to him, then, if need be, seeking help and guidance outside the family circle – but always from the "inside out", and always in that order. That's what the model for life is: doing things as Jesus would have done them. And this applies to all aspects of our lives; from decision-making, problem solving, moments of celebration, moments of sadness; no matter what, the model works.

Anytime you come to do something, simply ask yourself, 'How would Jesus have done it?' Then proceed as he would have, enlisting his help, and from there move outward."

"Does this make a little more sense now son?" asked Tommy.

"Much more sense," Pierre replied. "When you put it that way, life becomes less scary, and more of an adventure to find, with God's help, what lies around the next corner of life."

"Now you've got it!" exclaimed Tommy. "Life is ultimately a collaborative partnership between you and God, working hand in hand, to achieve the purpose for which He sent you. God will do His part; you simply have to do yours.

And on this journey, and in order to make it all the more successful, all the more enjoyable, He asks that you do only one thing: that you abide by the rules He has laid down for the journey, as He has dictated them: to obey and live by His commandments.

Do as Jesus did and success will overtake you beyond your wildest dreams.

With practice, prayer, supplication and obedience to God's commandments, you will become more comfortable with the idea. In time, as you do your part, life's journey will become a most exhilarating and joyous ride. So much so, that like the trapeze artist you mentioned earlier you will not only take delight in walking on life's high wire, but will be so confident in God as your safety net, that you will begin to do back-flips on your high wire, even when blindfolded.

God will open your eyes and help you make the connection between the things you do and the things He has planned for you.

Your strategic life plan is therefore simply this: to work with God to find His purpose for you; to use His Commandments as your Guiding Principles; and model your Operational Plan for getting there on Jesus.

Once you live life according to these terms, things like careers and success are guaranteed."

Chapter 6

Careers

Life And Careers

"Speaking of careers," Pierre asked, "did you always know what you wanted to be?"
"Not at first, and not for a long time," Tommy responded. "What I wanted to be evolved in stages. As a child I always felt I was destined to do something or be 'someone'. I never really knew what or who.
It was about my second year of high school before I got the first inkling as to the direction I should take.
It was summer holidays. I decided to take time out from a book I was reading and at mom's behest, set out to gather nutmegs from the field. It was about noon. There was not a cloud in the sky. The sun beat down upon the pavement and the heat rose from it, dancing like strings of flexible wire. Skylarks with wings outstretched, glided lazily in the skies above, oblivious to the inferno below. Sun beetles screeched, that piercing torturous screech, protesting the unrelenting and suffocating heat. Going into the garden then to do my chores, shaded by the trees, was a most welcome exercise.
Rod in hand, I moved from tree to tree, picking up the nuts that had already fallen and beating down those that were ripe but had not yet fallen to the ground.
At the half-way mark I sat down at the foot of a giant mango tree to rest. The tree and its neighbours had joined hands and the canopy of leaves extended into the heavens like a cathedral ceiling. As the wind rustled the leaves, the sun would sneak a peak and peer into the shade below. It was there that my thoughts of what I wanted to be began to take shape.

From an early age I was a voracious reader. I devoured as many books as I could find. A good story, just as the one I was reading at the time, always fascinated me. But just as fascinating to me were the letters behind the names of the people who wrote the books. The author of one of the books that I had read had the letters 'B.A.' at the end of his name. I remember thinking then, 'A B.A. must be important.'

And as I sat in the serenity of nature's cathedral, I said to myself: 'I'm going to get a B.A.' I didn't know what it meant, or what it entailed. It seemed an important thing to have, and I wanted one. So that was the genesis of my first step toward a career; my first goal: getting a B.A.

It would be many years before I achieved that first goal. My high school education had to be cut short because my younger brother, now of high school age, had to get his turn at high school. My mom, unable to afford fees for both of us, let me know that I had to leave school earlier than planned. I was disappointed, but understood.

At high school I was fortunate in having been given the opportunity to attempt the grade twelve exams in grade eleven, and to have passed some exams. So when I had to leave in grade twelve, a year before matriculation, I had had enough grade twelve subjects to at least allow me to get a job.

A few months before leaving school I sent out resumes to various banks and other institutions. I received only one response; from a bank inviting me to an interview. The day of the interview I put on my Sunday best and walked the short distance to the bank. Upon arrival, I approached the counter and introduced myself and the purpose for my visit. After a while I was ushered into the manager's office. As I entered the office, Mr. Beaver greeted me with an outstretched hand, while introducing himself to me. He then gestured for me to sit down. Mr. Beaver was a bespectacled man with discerning eyes. After we sat down he pulled out his pipe, opened a pouch of Amphora® tobacco, scooping some with the bowl of his pipe. After folding the pouch he struck a match and applied it to his pipe alternately sucking and puffing in quick short bursts. With each intake the tobacco would glow, and with each puff a cloud of smoke would rise and envelop his face.

With his pipe finally lit and with the aroma and smoke from the pipe rising in the air, the interview began. Mr. Beaver asked me about the courses I had taken, the activities in which I had participated in school. I was then given a test to complete.

I must have done well on the test, because after he had reviewed it, he remarked that I had done better than many of the grade thirteen graduates he had interviewed earlier.

As the interview came to an end Mr. Beaver had one final question, intended to gauge my commitment to the bank, should I be hired. He asked: 'What are your future plans?' I responded that my hope was to make banking a career. And then I added: 'The only reason I would ever leave the bank if hired, is to get a B.A.' The interview ended and I left.

On my way home I was hopeful, buoyed by my test results and the tenor of the interview.

After several weeks, a letter arrived from the bank. With trembling hands and a pounding heart, I opened it. It began: 'Dear Mr. Farnaby, it is with pleasure…' I got the job. I became a banker at eighteen, starting as a Teller.

After being silent for a while, Pierre asked: "Why didn't you make banking a career, dad?"

"It was one thing, really," Tommy replied. "It was because of the promise I made to myself to get a B.A.;

that promise pulled me away from banking. While I worked at the bank, it remained an unfulfilled yearning; and the longer I worked at the bank, the farther I seemed to drift from that goal.

As I approached my twenty-first birthday, the age at which, in our culture you reach adulthood, I became restless. I could not conceive of reaching adulthood and not having achieved my goal, or at least having started down the path to my goal. And so I committed to myself that on or before my twenty-first birthday, I had to set out in search of my dream. It meant that I had to leave home, since there were no universities on the island. So after three years at the bank, and four days after my twenty-first birthday, I set out in pursuit of my dream.

After my arrival in Canada and after much heartache, I landed the hospital job that allowed me to finish high school and enter university."

"Given the things you saw and did at the hospital, did you ever think of becoming a doctor?" Pierre asked.

"I actually did think about it, particularly after the head of gynecology said to me one day: 'You know Tommy, too bad you're not studying medicine. You would be a good doctor.'"

"Then why didn't you pursue it?" asked Pierre.

"Because I doubted whether I could be a good doctor. Not only that, I didn't have the academic prerequisites to study medicine. I had done reasonably well at Chemistry and some Math subjects; but I was lousy at Physics, and had never studied Biology or Bio-Chemistry or other prerequisites for medicine.

The gap between where I was and the goal of medicine was too wide for me to attempt it. It didn't mean that I couldn't become a doctor, because I believe we can be anything we want to be. It's just that the greater the gap between where you are and where you need to get to in any endeavour, the greater the effort required, the longer the time and the larger the store of resources needed to get there.

My lost high school years ate up some of that time, causing me to enter university at an age when my peers were already graduating. And although I worked around the hospital and was fascinated with the medical happenings around me, I was more fascinated by the sociological aspects of my environment. I was more drawn to the interactions within that microcosmic world, where like the Shakespearian world outside, people were born, they grew old and died.

The sciences were therefore less of a draw than the arts. Besides, the gap between where I was and my goal of achieving a B.A. was much narrower and provided greater leverage for me to succeed.

I discovered long ago that where there is a foundational connection between your present state and the state to which you aspire, your path to success becomes much easier. So I leveraged where I was and achieved my B.A. as planned."

"With your goal achieved, how did you move to the next phase?" Pierre asked.

"While a B.A. was my goal I didn't tie it to any particular career. So even after graduation, I still didn't know what I wanted to do. But no sooner had I graduated, when the business world beckoned again.

I spent several restless years in business. And while the restlessness in the early years at the bank had to do with my pursuit of a B.A., this new restlessness was more nebulous. It had to do with finding the right career fit, yet not knowing what that fit should be. True to form though, I did good work and over time got several promotions.

The longer I worked, the more I found that my greatest joy on the job was helping to transform others' lives; helping them to be the best they could be.

As financial services manager I also began to notice skill gaps in the young people coming out of school. I felt then that if this trend continued, sooner or later, companies would have to address this deficiency by creating the training facilities to fill the gaps.

I thought that it would be an area in which I would excel. So unlike my colleagues, I set out to pursue a M.Ed. in stead of a M.B.A., in preparation for the future.

After receiving my M.Ed. more and more of my job involved training and development. And as you know, it evolved to the point where I was traveling throughout the country, training and developing people.

Up to that point, I still hadn't identified my career, until one day, on Purdy's Wharf on the shores of Halifax, Nova Scotia.

I had gone east to train, and during a break in the session, as attendees streamed out, a few stopped to tell me how much they were enjoying the session. I stared out the window basking in the glow of the accolades. In the distance a ship was unloading its cargo. A ferry streamed by, cutting the water and leaving a frothy wake behind. Seagulls stood on an empty helipad preening themselves. Then it hit me: 'I'm a teacher!'

In all the years that I helped mom prepare for her kindergarten classes; cutting the paper, mixing and applying the glue to make papier-mâché objects, drawing stick men, I never thought of becoming a teacher. Nor had mom ever broached the question. Yet it seemed that all these years, as if by osmosis, I had acquired the skill, this love and penchant for teaching. Maybe it came about observing mom and the creative ways she taught. Maybe it was the sparkle I saw in her eyes and the satisfaction I saw in her face, when on a Sunday coming from church, she would be greeted by different people, many of them former students.

When she would inquire about what they did, some had become carpenters, some nurses, some teachers like her, some artists. And as I learned in later years, one even became prime minister.

So maybe it was the ability to transform lives that made a deep impression in me, creating a yearning to also make a difference.

But that yearning I believe goes far deeper than that. All of God's creations yearn. They have a deep desire to fulfill His purpose for them.

The grass seed that gets caught between the cracks in the sidewalk yearns for the day when it would break free. Imprisoned, it patiently waits for the opportunity. As the crack in the sidewalk widens, it finds room to grow. Then one day it seizes its opportunity and with flailing arms it waves triumphantly at having been able to break free and thrive.

"See those apple trees over there Pierre?" Tommy asked, pointing to the apple trees that lined the side of the house. "What do you notice about them?"

"They all seem to be leaning the same way; away from the house," Pierre replied.

"Do you know why?" Tommy continued.

"Not really," Pierre responded.

"Their leaning comes from their yearning to fulfill their purpose. They know that sunshine is vital to their survival and success, and so each day, when the sun shines, they strain and lean and reach toward the sunlight to get a taste of the elixir that would sustain them. That's why they lean away from the shade of the house, toward the light of the sun.

Like the grass seed, like the apple trees, we all have a purpose and yearn to fulfill it. Our yearning therefore, is merely a striving to uncover it. We do not have to figure it out. It has already been figured out for us. When a potter sits at his wheel to create a pot, he knows its purpose precisely. He creates it after his own fashion and marks it for its intended use. The pot has no say in its creation. Although it could be used for purposes other than what the potter intended, those other uses would never be as right, or fit as well as when it's being a pot.

So too with us; God determined our purpose long ago: 'For we are his workmanship, created in Christ Jesus for good works, which God prepared beforehand, that we should walk in them' [Ephesians 2:10].[1]

So our yearning like the grass seed or the apple tree is merely to seek, find and fulfill God's purpose for us. We miss that purpose more often than not, when we seek it from the 'outside in'. When we are driven to find that thing outside ourselves, that thing which we hope would give us fulfillment and satisfaction, we come up empty. When we find it, it gives us neither satisfaction nor fulfillment.

Lasting satisfaction and fulfillment only come when we begin our search from the 'inside out'. Since God created our purpose long ago, our search must start with Him. For 'Unless the Lord builds the house, those who build it labour in vain' [Psalm 127:1][2]

Unless we work from the 'inside out', we work in vain. So as we seek to fulfill God's purpose for us we must recognize and acknowledge that He already has the answer, and so to be successful, we must begin with a question to Him about the nature of that purpose.

If we simply do like the wind and the trees or the geese and simply hearken to His call; if we walk by faith and not by sight, we will find all that He has planned for us. So you should 'Take delight in the Lord, and he will give you the desires of your heart. Commit your way to the Lord; trust in him, and he will act.' [Psalm 37: 4-5].[3] Begin every endeavour from the 'inside out'. Until that day in Halifax, I missed that reality. As I uttered 'I'm a teacher!' it dawned on me that all along I had been what I was meant to be, and didn't know it."

"You mean you were on the path after all," said Pierre.

"Yes," replied Tommy. "I had been that trapeze artist you talked about, with a safety net I didn't know I had. All the elements of life we talked about had converged to bring me to my purpose: my commitment to faith and all that it required of me; my obedience to and shaping by my mom; my own efforts. All converged to culminate in that purpose".

"That's why I'm telling you this story," Tommy continued. "I want you to know that God indeed guides you to His desired purpose for you. Only this time, and through this conversation, I want you to be conscious of His working in you. Continue to do all we talked about, follow Jesus's example and all will be well with you. Life's purpose, after all, is as much a search as it is a discovery. Just as the potter gives the pot all it needs to function; so too God gives us all we need: the right place of birth, the right parents, the right environment, and the right gifts.[4]

Begin your search from the 'inside out'. First query God about His purpose for you; then look to your immediate family for signs of His purpose and follow as He guides you. The answer is usually right where you live, or within the family tree.

It is no surprise therefore that the children of doctors become doctors; the children of actors, actors and the children of teachers, teachers.

They may not be doctors in the same field or teachers in the same environment. They may even become variations of their parents' or grand parents' professions or calling, but the influence would be unmistakable.

The influence of my grand- parents' business background and my mom's teaching influence, combined to help me become a teaching business man. I can't help but think that even if I had become a doctor, I would have taught medicine; and if I had become a lawyer, I would have taught law. The pull to transform lives through teaching is too great to have been ignored.

If I had known in my early years what I discovered in Halifax, and the power of living from the 'inside out', I would have taken greater delight in the journey. When you know that your purpose in life is already established, it takes away all the pressure from living. Life becomes a journey of discovery and excitement; a labour of love; a joy ride, just as the song I used to sing to you when you were younger:

Row, row, row your boat
Gently down the stream
Merrily, merrily, merrily, merrily
Life is but a dream

This metaphor for life depicts perfectly, what the journey should look like:

Life requires work: 'Row, Row, Row…'

It requires accountability: 'Your Boat…'

It requires you to work with life's currents: 'Gently down the stream…'

And you are expected to enjoy the ride: 'Merrily. Merrily, merrily…' in the discovery of your dream."

Epilog

Just as Tommy finished speaking the street lights across the street flickered and came on, casting a dull orange glow upon the landscape. The darkness that now enveloped them had long chased the sun from the sky. A sliver of a moon struggled to rise above the dark clouds around it.
Tommy, sensing that Pierre was tired said to him: "Your success will continue as long as you live from the 'inside out' son. Love God. Write His commandments on a piece of paper. Then write them on your memory, then on your heart and on your lips. Live by them. Speak to Jesus every day and through him to his Father.
Thank him when he blesses you. Speak to him often in good times, so that he will recognize your voice when you call him in times of trouble".

After a brief silence, Pierre eased to his six foot frame, and with the wing span of a '747' he embraced his dad and squeezed him as only he could squeeze.
"Thanks dad," he whispered. "Today was wonderful. Please promise me that you would write everything down, please."
"I promise," Tommy replied.
"Thanks," Pierre responded.
"Good night dad."
"Good night son."

Resources

1. The Purpose Driven® Life
Copyright © 2002 Rick Warren
International Trade Paper Edition

2. The Holy Bible
Revised Standard Version
London Catholic truth Society
© 1965
Published by Thomas Nelson & Sons Ltd

References

Chapter 1: Life from the Inside Out

1. Matthew 6:9-13
2. Mark 12:28-30
3. The Purpose Driven® Life P. 17
4. Exodus 3:13-14
5. Hebrews 11:1

Chapter 2: The Real Life Connection

1. Deuteronomy 28:1-6

Chapter 3: Love from the Inside Out

1. John 14:13
2. 1 Corinthians 13:4-7

Chapter 4: Success from the Inside Out

1. Matthew 25:14-29
2. John 2:1-11
3. Mark 10:17-20
4. Deuteronomy 5:6-21
5. Matthew 6:31-33

Chapter 5: Jesus as Model

1. John 15:10
2. Matthew 22:36-37
3. Deuteronomy 6:4-5
4. Matthew 4:4
5. Deuteronomy 8:3
6. Mark 1:35
7. John 17:9-10

8. Luke 10:21
9. Mark 14:22-23
10. Luke 22:44
11. John 14:13
12. Luke 23:34
13. Luke 3:46-47
14. Matthew 5:1-12
15. Matthew 22:16-21
16. Mark 7:36-37
17. John 21:9-12
18. Luke 12:22-23

Chapter 6: Careers

1. Ephesians 2:10
2. Psalm 127:1
3. Psalm 37:4-5
4. The Purpose Driven® Life PP 22-24

Appendix A – Life From The Inside Out

1. Getting My Head Around God

2. Getting My Head Around Jesus

3. Getting My Heart Around Jesus

Complete the exercises that follow by circling the relevant letter.
Your responses will help identify and prioritize areas of growth.
For each area needing improvement, outline a personal improvement plan.
Legend:
a = always
s = sometimes
n = never

Appendix A – Exercises – Life From The Inside Out

1. I begin each day with prayer a s n

2. I end each day with prayer a s n

3. I always start with God when making decisions a s n

4. After seeking God's help I then look to see what I could do to make things happen a s n

5. I also look to family as my next step in decision-making a s n

6. My family's opinion of me is as favourable as the opinions of strangers about me a s n

7. I have succeeded in getting my head around God a s n

8. I have experienced several memorable events that helped me get my head around God a s n

9. I have succeeded in getting my head around Jesus a s n

10. Real life experiences have helped me get my heart Around Jesus a s n

11. Each day I look for and find validation of God's active presence in my life a s n

Appendix A – Exercises – Life From The Inside Out

Developing A Relationship With God	
Areas Needing Improvement	**Things I will do to improve**

Appendix A – Notes – Life From The Inside Out

Appendix B – The Real Life Connection

1. What kids need to know

2. What parents need to know

3. What teachers need to know

4. What our Black Lab taught me

Complete the exercises that follow by circling the relevant letter.
Your responses will help identify and prioritize areas of growth.
For each area needing improvement, outline a personal improvement plan.
Legend:
a = always
s = sometimes
n = never

Appendix B – Exercises – The Real Life Connection

1. I honour my parents	a	s	n
2. I show my parents love, respect and obedience in all that is right	a	s	n
3. I honour my grandparents	a	s	n
4. I show my grandparents love, respect and obedience in all that is right	a	s	n
5. I help around the house	a	s	n
6. When I help I do so cheerfully and willingly	a	s	n
7. I make a difference at home	a	s	n
8. I make a difference in my school community	a	s	n
9. I make a difference in the community at large	a	s	n
10. I ask Jesus for help in everything I do	a	s	n
11. I expect his help when I ask	a	s	n
12. He responds to my prayers	a	s	n

13. As a parent, I believe that my obedience to God's Commandments yields blessings not only for me but also for my children a s n

14. I practice living from the inside out a s n

15. I teach my children to live from the inside out a s n

16. I lead by both precept and example a s n

17. As a teacher, I accept that I'm accountable to God and responsible for my role in Shaping the lives of children a s n

18. I am conscious of the lasting impact my teaching has on children a s n

19. I give my best efforts in serving God's people a s n

20. I lead by precept and example a s n

21. I believe that God is active And alive in my life and in the world a s n

22. I find God in every-day experiences Of life a s n

Appendix B – Exercises – The Real Life Connection

Connecting Living With God	
Areas Needing Improvement	**Things I will do to improve**

Appendix B – Notes – The Real Life Connection

Appendix C – Love From The Inside Out

1. Life and Love

2. A Letter of Love

Complete the exercises that follow by circling the relevant letter.
Your responses will help identify and prioritize areas of growth.
For each area needing improvement, outline a personal improvement plan.
Legend:
a = always
s = sometimes
n = never

Appendix C – Exercises – Love From The Inside Out

1. I do love God	a	s	n
2. I obey His Commandments	a	s	n
3. I practice all the characteristics of love as described by Paul	a	s	n
4. I do love myself as Paul expresses love	a	s	n
5. I do love my family	a	s	n
6. I have expressed my love to those around me	a	s	n
7. I do love my neighbours	a	s	n

Appendix C – Exercises – Love From The Inside Out

Practicing Love	
Areas Needing Improvement	**Things I will do to improve**

Appendix C – Notes – Love From The Inside Out

Appendix D – Success From The Inside Out

1. A Catalyst for success

2. Honour your father and your mother

3. The Rich Young Man

4. Practice, Practice, Practice

5. Do More Than The bare Minimum

6. Look, Listen and Shut Your Mouth

7. Look for and Find Opportunities for Success

8. Do all things well

9. Avoid Living by Exception

10. Do not be an Eye Servant

11. Failure is an Option

12. Take care of Today – Tomorrow will take care of itself

13. Life is like an Automatic Door

14. Live Life with a Willing Spirit

15. Finish Everything you start

16. The Power of Education

17. The Power of Thanks

18. Courtesy

19. Character

Complete the exercises that follow by circling the relevant letter.
Your responses will help identify and prioritize areas of growth.
For each area needing improvement, outline a personal improvement plan.
Legend:
a = always
s = sometimes
n = never

Appendix D – Exercises – Success From The Inside Out

1. I have encountered significant events for success in my life	a	s	n
2. I have used those events as motivation to succeed	a	s	n
3. I have been influenced by those around me to succeed	a	s	n
4. I have acted on those influences	a	s	n
5. I honour my parents and guardians	a	s	n
6. I respect the judgment of my parents and guardians	a	s	n
7. I obey my parents and guardians in all that is right	a	s	n
8. I obey the Ten Commandments	a	s	n
9. I believe that following the Ten Commandments will lead me to success like the Rich Young Man	a	s	n
10. I constantly practice whatever I do	a	s	n
11. I believe that constant practice will bring me success	a	s	n
12. I do more than I'm asked to	a	s	n

13. I observe, listen and learn	a	s	n
14. I ask relevant questions	a	s	n
15. I survey my surroundings to find opportunities for success	a	s	n
16. I do all things well	a	s	n
17. I live by exception	a	s	n
18. I believe that living by exception will hinder my success	a	s	n
19. I am an eye servant	a	s	n
20. I need praise and outside stimulus to do good work	a	s	n
21. I view failure as a learning experience	a	s	n
22. If I fail anything I review where I failed and make the necessary corrections	a	s	n
23. I never leave for tomorrow, the things I can do today	a	s	n
24. I see life as an automatic door – I Move successfully from goal to goal	a	s	n
25. I do everything willingly and cheerfully	a	s	n

26. I learn in life, by
finishing everything I start a s n

27. I love to learn a s n

28. I believe in the power
of Education a s n

29. I always seek to up-grade my skills and
level of education a s n

30. I strive to attain the highest level of education
available to me a s n

31. I thank God for what I receive a s n

32. I make sure I thank those around me
who help me a s n

33. I am courteous a s n

34. I act with integrity a s n

35. My behavior is beyond reproach a s n

Appendix D – Exercises – Success From The Inside Out

Practicing Success	
Areas Needing Improvement	**Things I will do to improve**

Appendix D – Exercises – Success From The Inside Out

Practicing Success	
Areas Needing Improvement	**Things I will do to improve**

Appendix D – Exercises – Success From The Inside Out

Practicing Success	
Areas Needing Improvement	**Things I will do to improve**

Appendix D – Exercises – Success From The Inside Out

Practicing Success	
Areas Needing Improvement	**Things I will do to improve**

Appendix D – Notes – Success From The Inside Out

Appendix D – Notes – Success From The Inside Out

Appendix D – Notes – Success From The Inside Out

Appendix E – Jesus As Model

1. He loved honoured and obeyed his Father

2. He studied the word

3. He prayed often

4. He prayed for others

5. He gave thanks in prayer

6. He prayed when anguished

7. He invited us to pray for whatever we need

8. He forgave those who wronged him – he bore no grudges

9. He loved his neighbor

10. He was a curious learner

11. He was an orator

12. He showed deference to authority

13. Excellence was his hallmark

14. He was Multi-Talented

Complete the exercises that follow by circling the relevant letter.
Your responses will help identify and prioritize areas of growth.
For each area needing improvement, outline a personal improvement plan.

Appendix E

Legend:
a = always
s = sometimes
n = never

Appendix E – Exercises – Jesus as Model

1. Jesus in my model for life	a	s	n
2. I love honour and obey him	a	s	n
3. I study the Bible as Jesus did	a	s	n
4. I pray often	a	s	n
5. I pray for others	a	s	n
6. I give thanks in prayer	a	s	n
7. I pray when troubled	a	s	n
8. I pray for whatever I need	a	s	n
9. I forgive those who wrong me	a	s	n
10. I bear no grudges	a	s	n
11. I love my neighbour	a	s	n
12. I am a curious learner	a	s	n
13. I love to learn	a	s	n
14. I love to share what I know with others	a	s	n
15. I am a life-long learner	a	s	n
16. I am a good communicator	a	s	n
17. I show deference to authority	a	s	n

18. I do all things well	a	s	n
19. I believe in being versatile	a	s	n
20. I use my many talents	a	s	n

Appendix E – Exercises – Jesus as Model

Practicing To Be Like Jesus	
Areas Needing Improvement	**Things I will do to improve**

Appendix E – Exercises – Jesus as Model

Practicing To Be Like Jesus	
Areas Needing Improvement	**Things I will do to improve**

Appendix E – Exercises – Jesus as Model

Practicing To Be Like Jesus	
Areas Needing Improvement	**Things I will do to improve**

Appendix E – Exercises – Jesus as Model

Practicing To Be Like Jesus	
Areas Needing Improvement	**Things I will do to improve**

Appendix E – Notes – Jesus as Model

Appendix E – Notes – Jesus as Model

Appendix E – Notes – Jesus as Model

Appendix F – Careers

1. Life and careers

Complete the exercises that follow by circling the relevant letter.
Your responses will help identify and prioritize areas of growth.
For each area needing improvement, outline a personal improvement plan.
Legend:
a = always
s = sometimes
n = never

Appendix F – Exercises – Careers

1. I believe I have a purpose a s n

2. I believe that God determined my purpose long ago a s n

3. I constantly ask God to lead me to His purpose for me a s n

4. I first look to God for career guidance a s n

5. I actively look for clues to His guidance a s n

6. I am able to validate His guidance a s n

7. I act according to His guidance a s n

8. I then look to my family tree for potential career examples a s n

9. I set goals that are **SMART** [**S**pecific, **M**easurable, **A**ttainable, **R**ealistic, and **T**ime-Bound] a s n

10. I constantly check on my progress toward my goals a s n

11. I make the necessary adjustments to my plan a s n

12. I keep a record of my successes and set-backs along the way	a	s	n
13. I use my successes and set-backs as motivators	a	s	n
14. I use my successes and set-backs as lessons to propel me toward my goals	a	s	n
15. I am enjoying life's journey	a	s	n
16. I am rowing my boat gently down the stream of life	a	s	n
17. On this journey I always row from the "inside out"	a	s	n

Appendix F – Exercises – Careers

Practicing To Find My Purpose	
Areas Needing Improvement	**Things I will do to improve**

Appendix F – Exercises – Careers

Practicing To Find My Purpose	
Areas Needing Improvement	**Things I will do to improve**

Appendix F – Exercises – Careers

Practicing To Find My Purpose	
Areas Needing Improvement	**Things I will do to improve**

Appendix F – Exercises – Careers

Practicing To Find My Purpose	
Areas Needing Improvement	**Things I will do to improve**

Appendix F – Notes – Careers

Appendix F – Notes – Careers

Appendix F – Notes – Careers

Index

www.ingramcontent.com/pod-product-compliance
Ingram Content Group UK Ltd.
Pitfield, Milton Keynes, MK11 3LW, UK
UKHW021053270726
13967UKWH00012B/638